AF266140

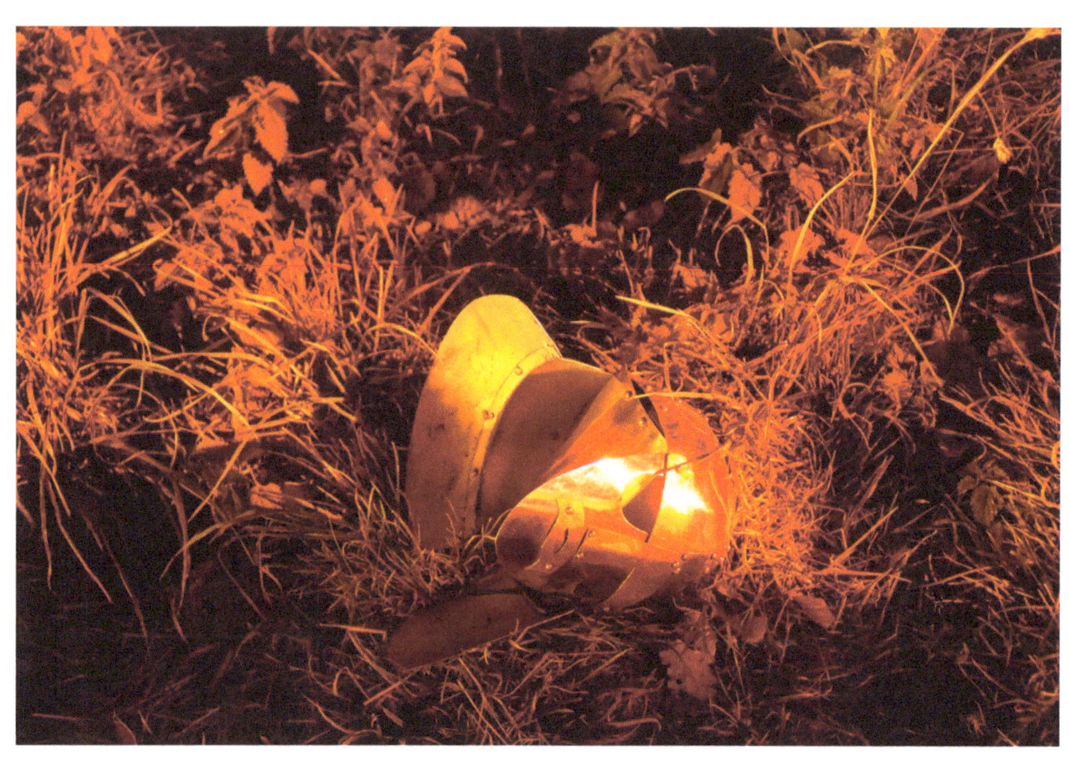

After the Fire 2016

Bonfire - A Journey

Teresa Neal

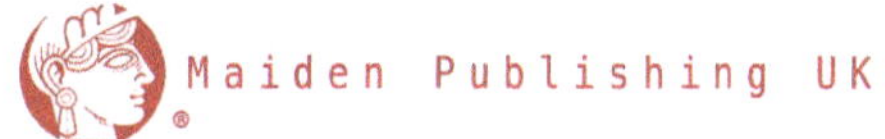

Maiden Publishing UK

Bonfire - A Journey

Frontispiece *Fire Ring*

By Teresa Neal

Published by Maiden Publishing
Phone: 05603643902
Email: info@maidenpublishing.co.uk
https://maidenpublishing.co.uk

First Edition 2021- ISBN 978-0-9928500-67

Disclaimer

Contents

Preface

There are about forty-three bonfire societies in Sussex, forty-nine including all the Lewes societies.The bonfire festivals run from September to November each year, the celebrations mark both Guy Fawkes night and the burning of the seventeen protestant martyrs in Lewes during Mary Tudors reign.

However, bonfire has its roots in social unrest and protest when torches were burnt and bonfires lit to show discontent. Later bonfires were banned as a form of protest when former Lewes bonfire boy Tom Paine started the Chartists and moved towards peaceful protest and lobbying. Consequently the 5th November became the only night of the year people could continue the working class tradition of protesting by lighting bonfires and burning effigies which was allowed on 5th November under the auspices of the *Observance of November 5th Act.*

By 1827 the Bonfire Boys and gangs had become more organised darkening their faces to avoid recognition and arrest. The tar barrels associated with Lewes bonfire were introduced in 1832 when they were sent blazing down the wealthy timber streets of Lewes, in an open threat to the rich and their property. This continued until 1846 when a local magistrate was knocked unconscious while trying to call the crowd to order, which caused the authorities to act. The London Police were called to Lewes and Henry Pelham, 3rd Earl of Chichester read the Riot Act on the steps of Lewes county hall after a night of fighting, and the crowds were roughly dispersed. However, the Bonfire Boys remained undefeated and celebrated the following night, the celebrations spreading to other parts of Sussex and continuing for the rest of November. Following this bonfire celebrations were no longer called riots and deemed to be a tradition in 1848 it was agreed that Wallands Park become the site of the festivities.

I came late to bonfire, discovering it in 2011 when the Seaford Shags reformed after disbanding in the 1970's. After witnessing the procession and firework display a friend persuaded me to join Seaford Bonfire Society in 2012.

I was captivated by the cultural, social and historical aspects of the tradition and the wonder it inspired in both those who take part and the spectators. As I became part of the 'bonfire family' I was struck by the high level of dedication of those involved in staging the event, especially by those who were born into bonfire and had always known it. In 2018 I became more involved behind the scenes of the event, because I felt I needed to know how the event came into being. I created the societies website in 2018 and became part of the firesite team. The firesite team are responsible for creating the bonfire and preparing the site for the night.

Drawn in by the spectacle I embarked upon a photographic journey. The photographs in this book capture my experiences of Seaford Bonfire Society together with images caught while visiting other bonfire nights during 'out meetings.' Bonfire appeals to our senses, as it lights the darkness, the warmth of the fire contrasting with the bitter night and damp air, together with the mist and the musky smell created by the gunpowder and smoke. It is this feeling that I have sought to bring to my photography in order to bring to life the atmosphere of the event, using a reportage style of photography to document the proceedings.

Some of the images have received awards from international competitions such as The color Awards and PX3. The Sussex Express also wrote a piece about my award-winning work *Stoking the Fire* in 2017.

In *Bonfire - A Journey*, the bonfire experience is laid out from the earliest preparation to the end product, not forgetting some of the people and characters that make the night what it is.

About the Artist

Teresa Neal is a multi-award winning artist who has exhibited internationally. She chooses to explore her central themes of loss and identity through working in a variety of ways using both documentary and artistic photography. Thematically Teresa explores loss, identity, death, memento-mori, class division and environmental decay. She has an intense awareness of how humans misuse their time and exploit both the environment and one another.

Photography had always been part of Teresa's practice and in 2004 she decided to focus on it, as moving away from the larger scale work she had been doing. Digital photography had started to come to the fore and the immediacy and accessibility of this new type of photography seemed to be the perfect vehicle to explore and experiment with new ideas.

Below is a selected list of Teresa's exhibitions.

Artbox the Stricoff Gallery New York group exhibition 5th - 16th March 2018
Light & Dark - A group black and white video and photography projection I organised for Photohastings at Sussex Coast College 4th floor gallery.
In the Eye of Noir 2017 - Solo exhibition at the Crypt art Gallery of black and white photography on the theme of fear and phobia. The show was accompanied by a book launch, workshop and artists talk.
Any Colour as Long as it's Orange, Photohastings 2016 - I Organised and curated an outdoor exhibition at Bottle Alley based on the perceptive experience of Neil Harbisson the colour blind artist who sees all skin tones as orange
Nakashirke Gallery Moscow - A group show of physical and projected work for MIFA winners in Russia.
MIFA Best of Show- My work travelled with the best of show to FotoLoft Moscow in 2014 and the Rooftop Gallery Bangkok 2014
SwissFoto13 - An international photography exhibition at the Swiss Art Space Lausanne exhibited *Smugglers Fire*
Miami Biennale 2013 - Biennale included the main exhibition at Miami Ironside, a digital display at the Campus Collective by Artists for Artists and an auction.
Naples Museum of Fine Art Florida 2013 - My artwork was auctioned and displayed at the charity benefit Incognito 2013.
Georgian National Gallery of Fine Arts 2012 - June 10-21 exhibited four large scale works as part of the International Exhibition sponsored by the ministry of culture, of Digital Art and Photography held at the Tbilisi Shalva Amiranashvili Museum.
Grishasvili History Museum Georgia 2011 - I took part in the first international exhibition of digital art and photography entitled Europe Seeking New Identity which took place between the 9th-16th May in honour of Europe Day.
Brighton Fringe 2011 - I took part in the worlds third largest fringe festival exhibiting landscape and portrait photography at the AM Gallery Brighton.
Photographers Gallery 2007 - My work part of a montage accompanying Helen Marshalls project *What Haunts You,* in the In Focus Gallery.
8th Hellenic Festival 2006 - My work was chosen to be exhibited as part of a digital display at the Athens festival of artistic photography.
Croydon Clocktower 2000
I exhibited a large aluminium hanging sculpture in the foyer called *The Three Muses* based on the three ages of womanhood.
Mini Galleries 2000
Shoe Stairway, the assemblage, toured the Mini Gallery sites of: Fairfield Halls, Mayday Hospital and Croydon Clocktower.

IN MEMORY OF RO… & VERA COOPER

DIONNE, ETHAN & PIPER DAVI…

IN MEMORY OF KEN & GILL HONEYWOOD

MICHAEL JOHN EVEREST 1983/2012

IN MEMORY OF A WONDERFUL DAD & GRANDPA, BILL HUGHES

IN MEMORY OF GEORGE PETTITT

THE HOUSE FAMILY IN MEMORY OF IAN McALLISTER

IN MEMORY OF DAVID GEORGE

IN MEMORY OF PAULINE REED & LINDSAY POCCACHARD

IN MEMORY OF EVA PRIOR

MR T FRANKS

SANDRA & ANDREW

ANDREW & ROGER

IN MEMORY OF SONNY & JOAN PLAYFORD

IN MEMORY OF BRIAN OWEN

ARTWORK

FIREWORK 20

IAN

IN MEMORY OF MAURICE EDWIN "TED" COOPER

IN MEMORY OF DIESEL

THE HOUSE FAMILY IN MEMORY OF SLYVIA PULLINGER

HAPPY 7TH BIRTHDAY ISLA ROBINSON

IN MEMORY OF SHEBA & SOPHIE

JAMES & ARON BURFIELD

THE WOODGATE FAMILY

SPONSORS 19

TERESA NEAL

IN MEMORY OF MARGERY KYME

Preparation

"Every man's work, whether it be literature or music or pictures or architecture or anything else, is always a portrait of himself, and the more he tries to conceal himself the more clearly will his character appear in spite of him."

Samuel Butler,

The Way of All Flesh

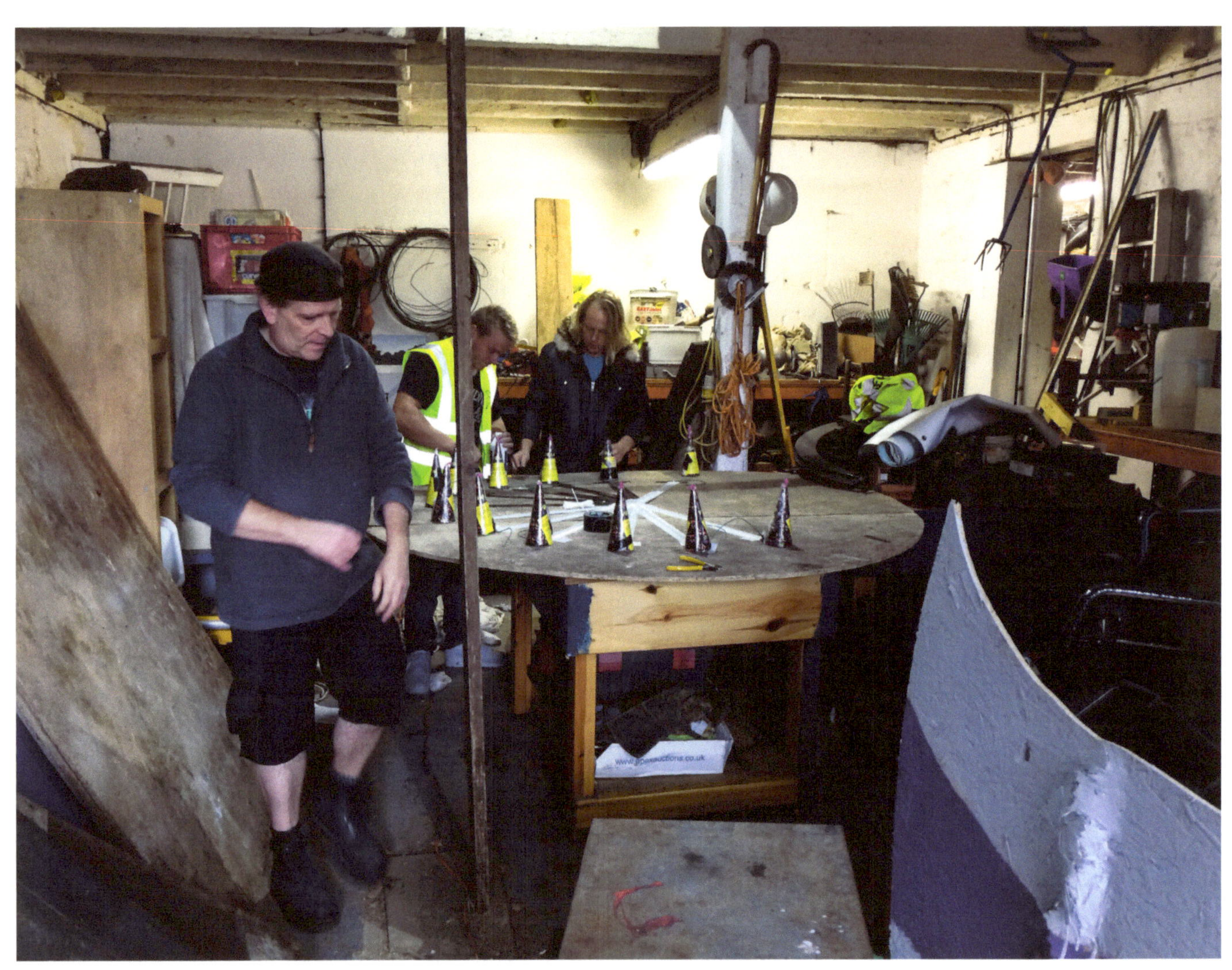

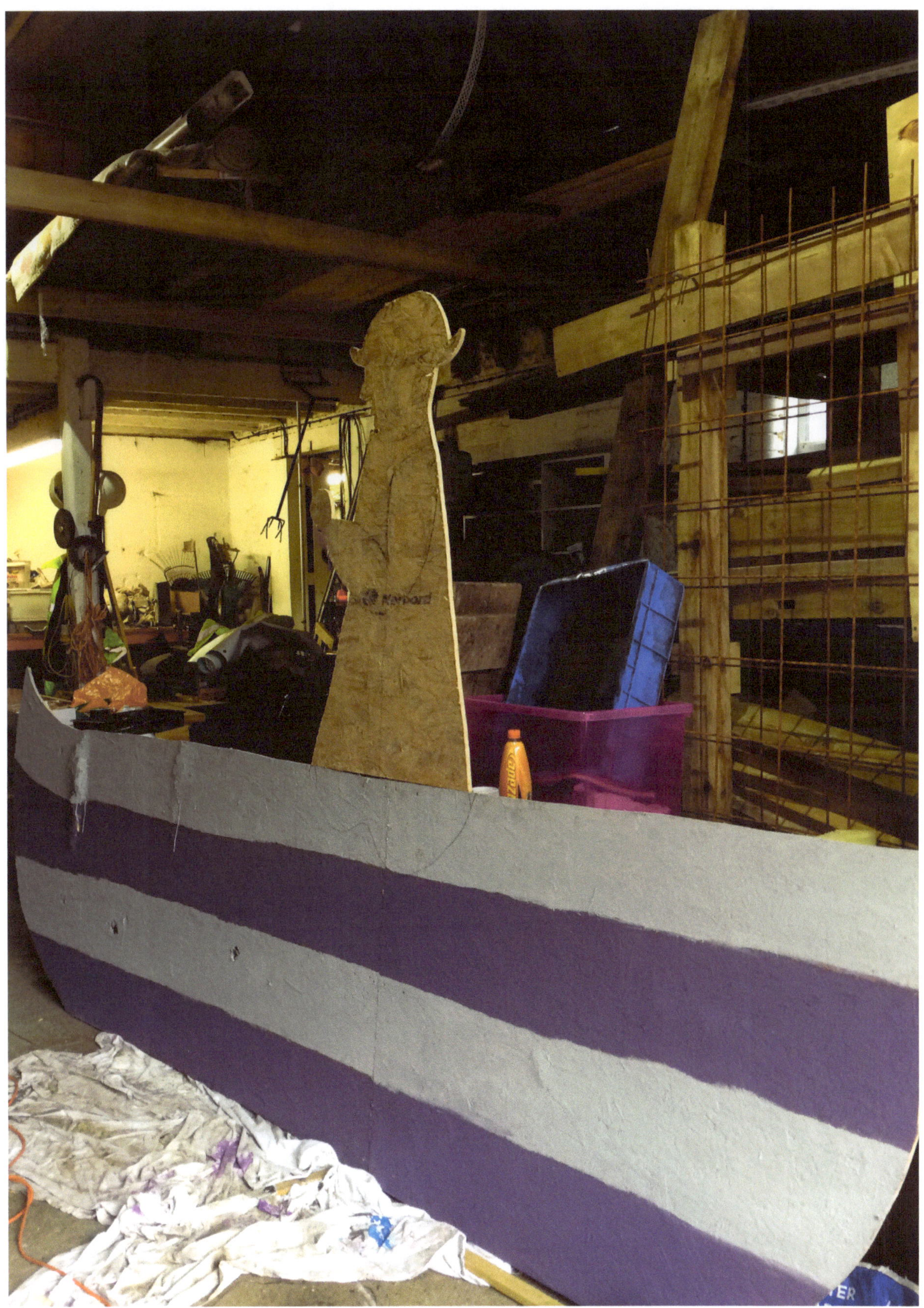

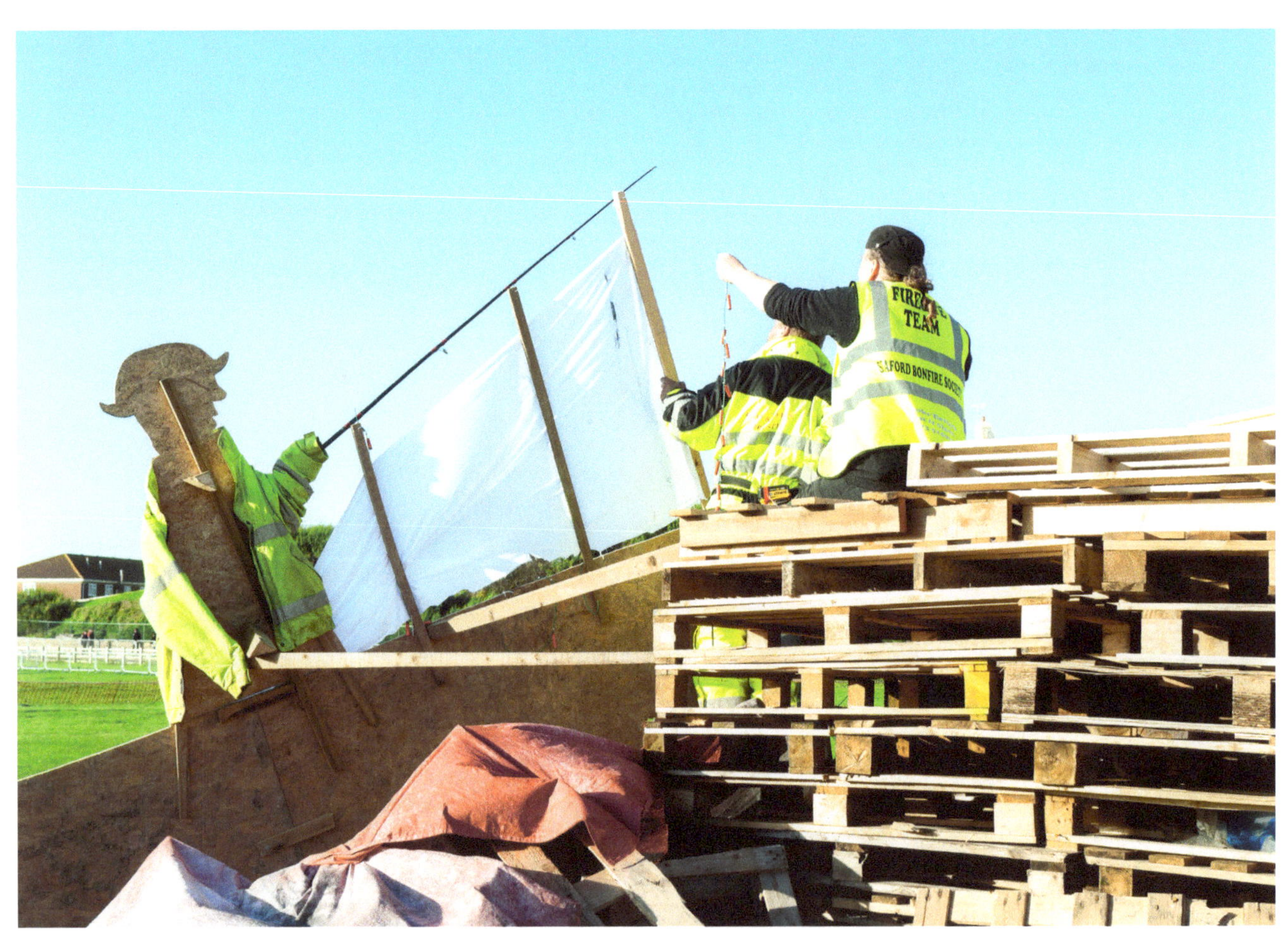

FIRE TEAM
TEAM
SEAFORD BONFIRE SOCIETY

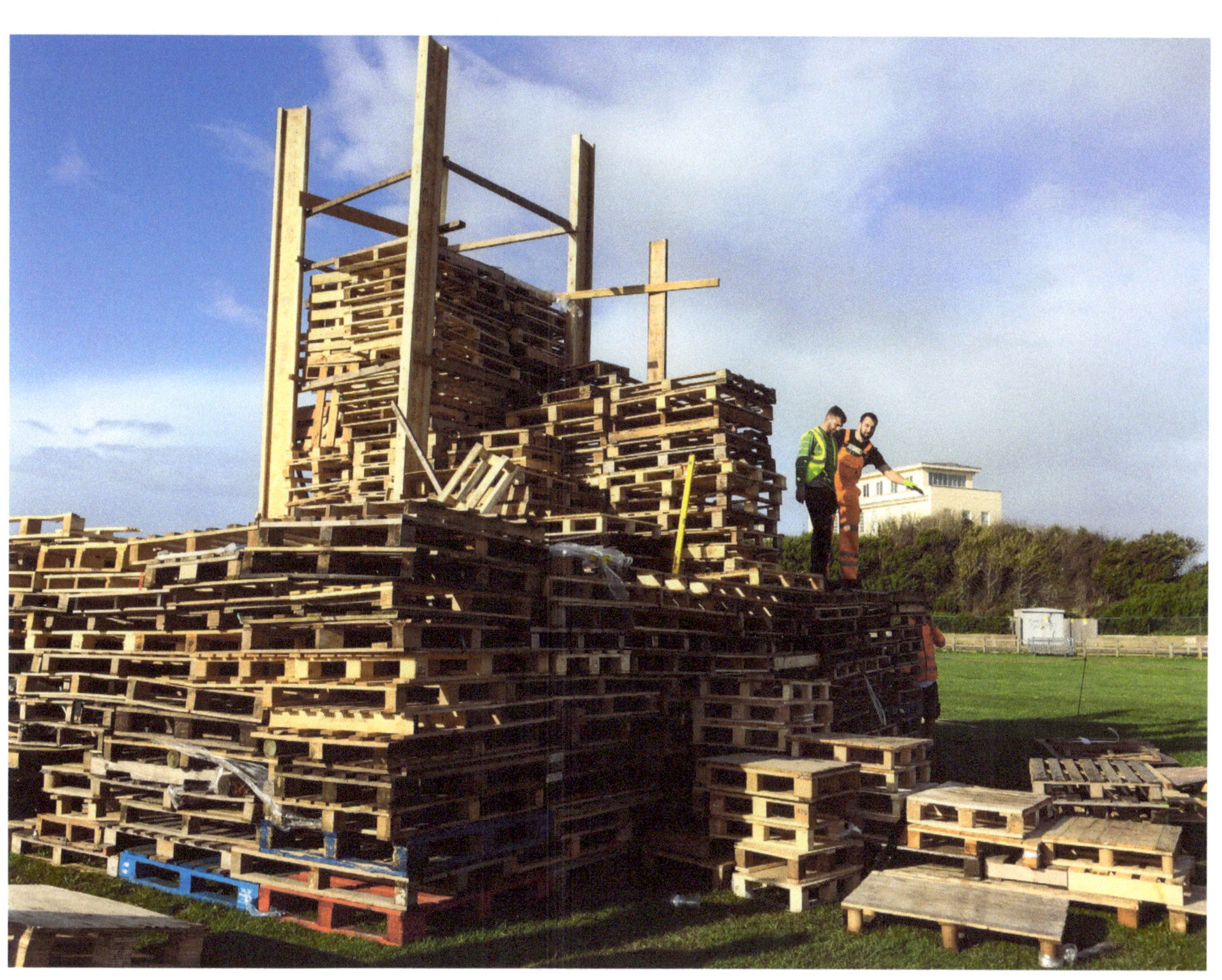

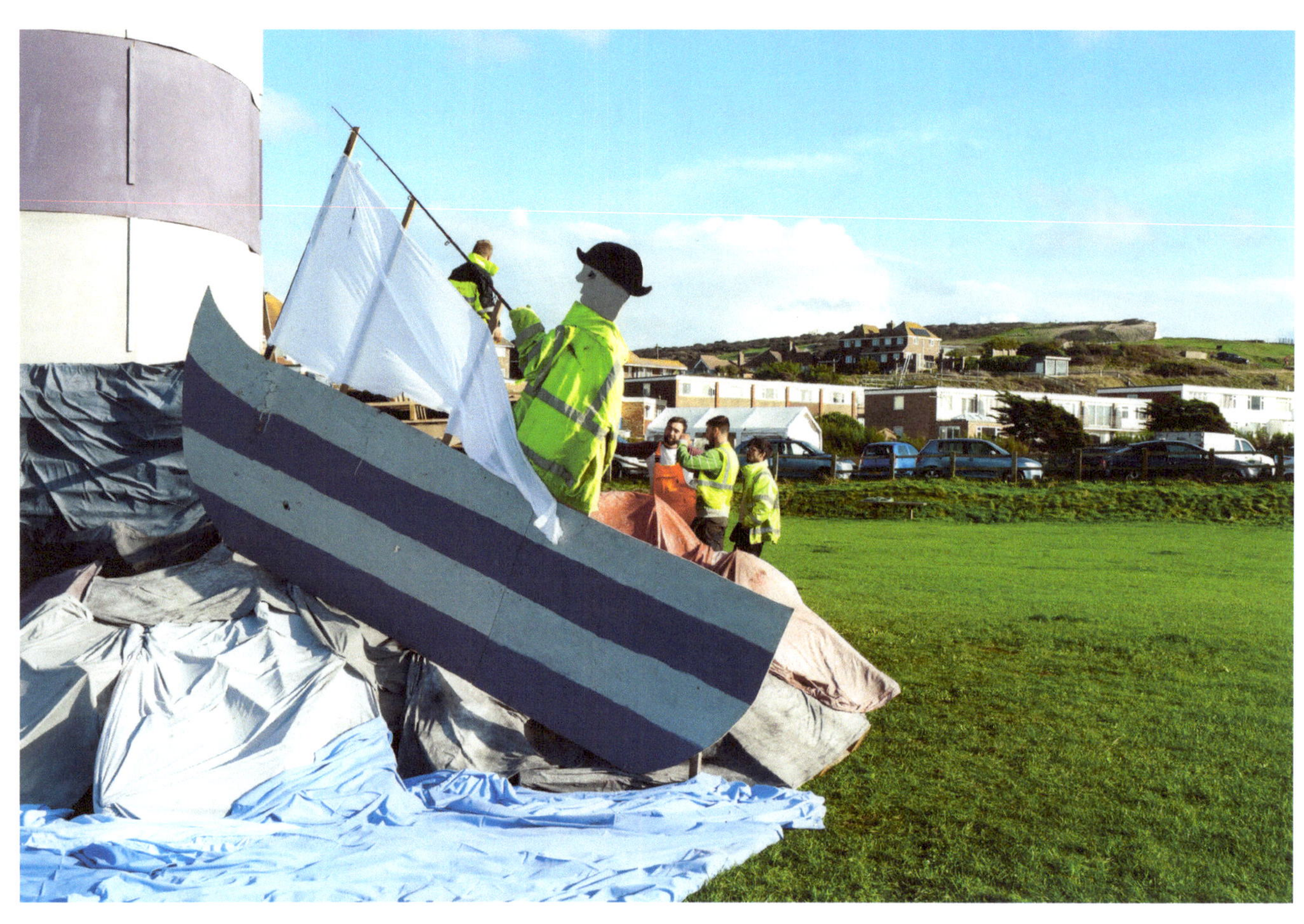

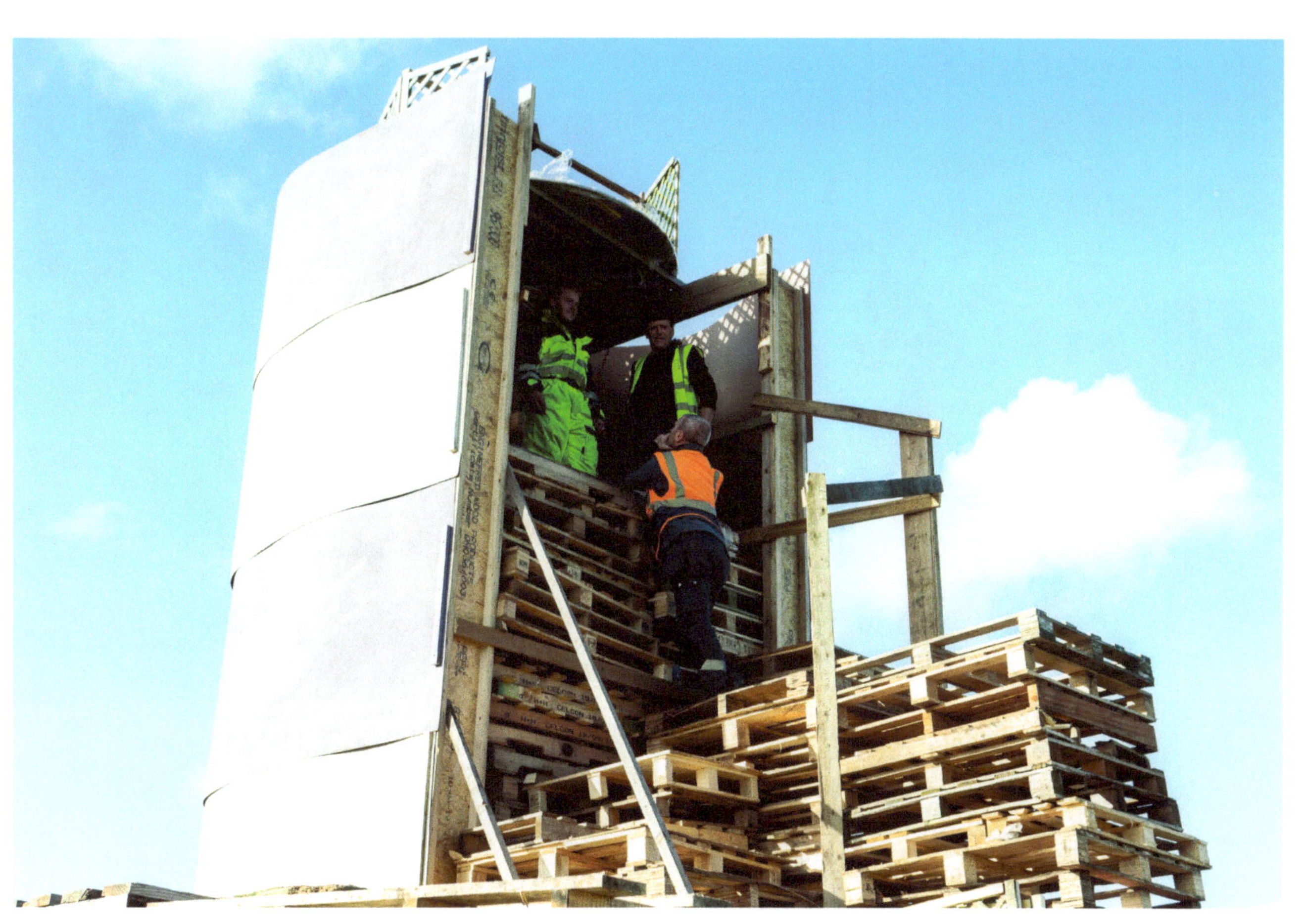

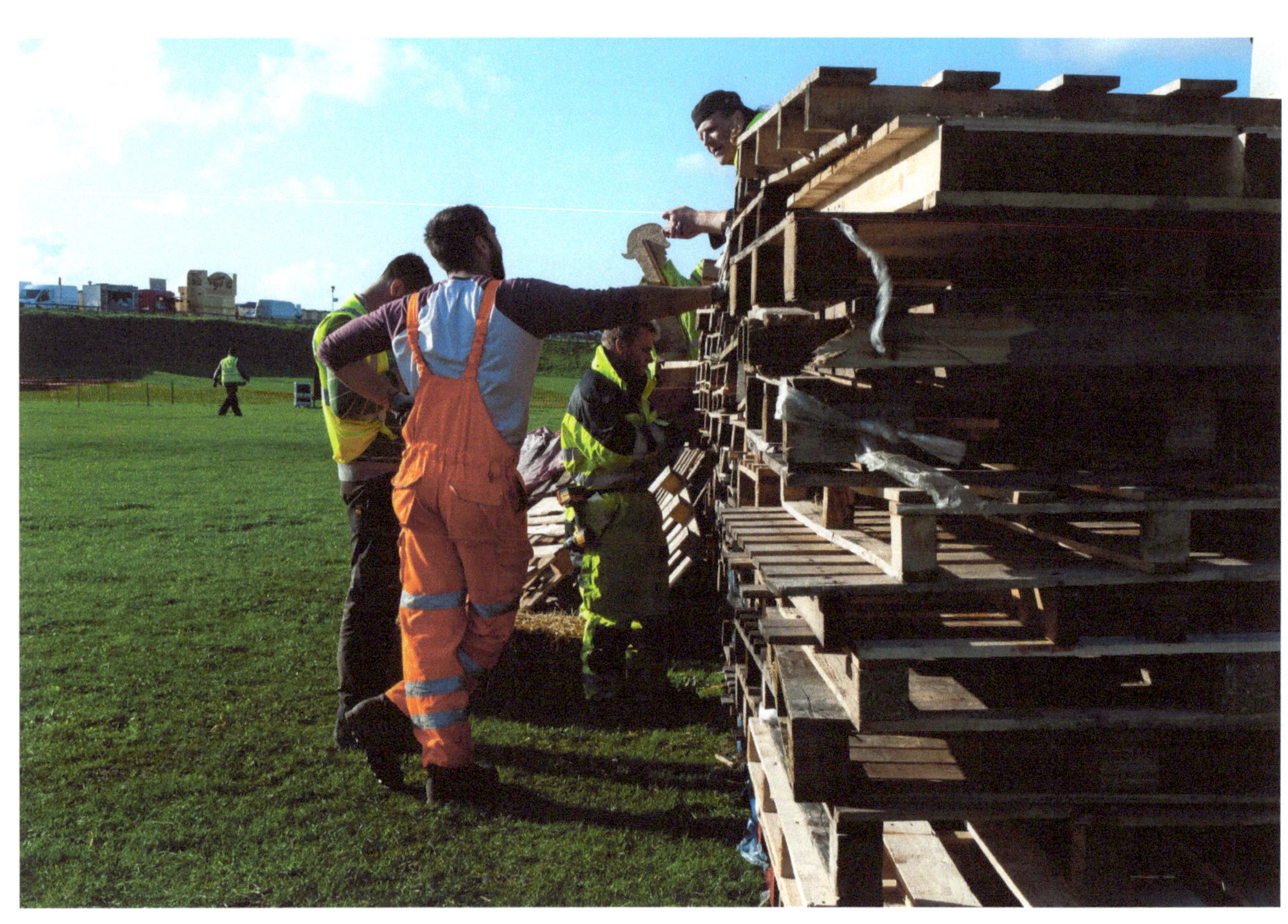

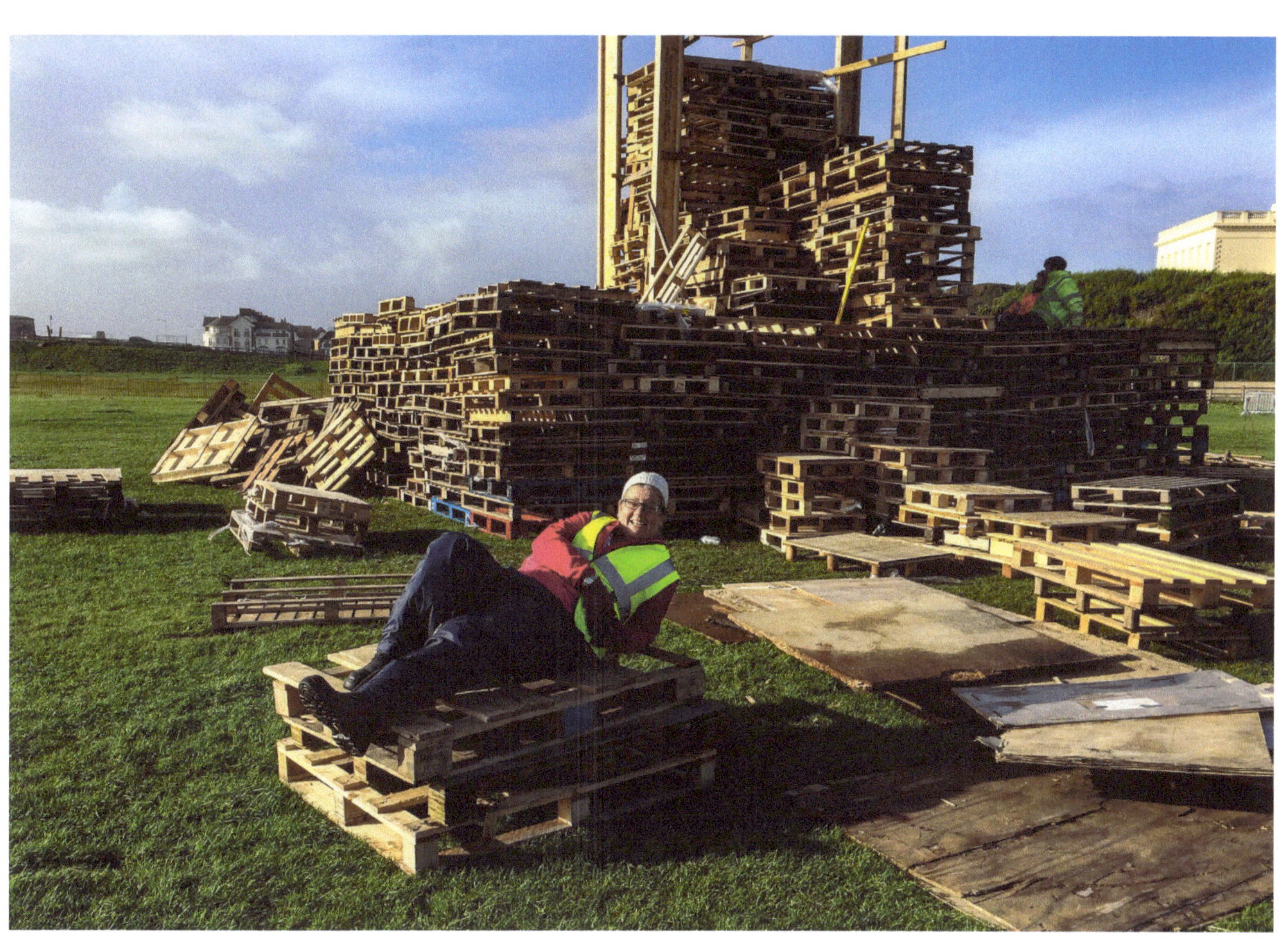

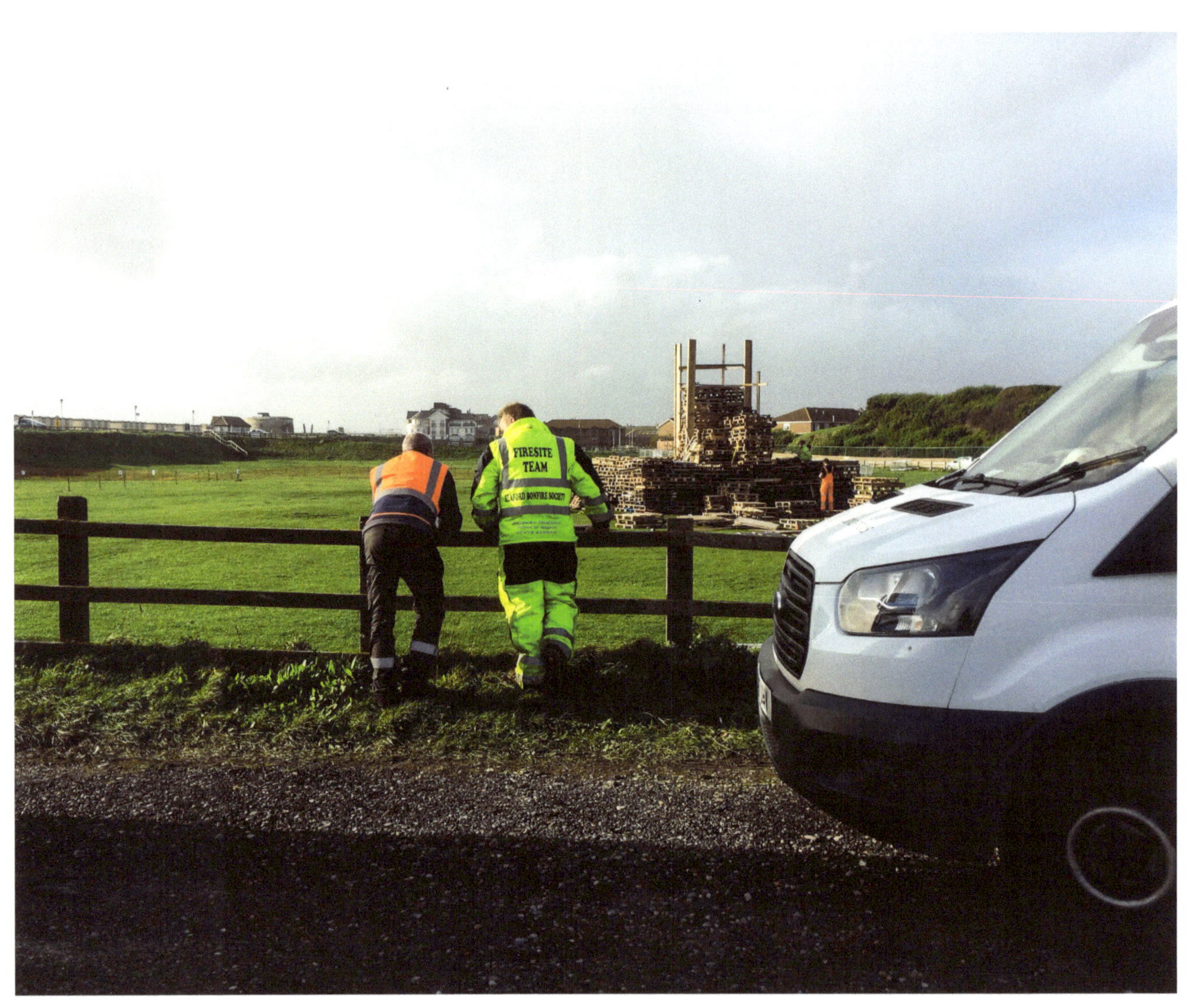
FIRESITE
TEAM
SEAFORD BONFIRE SOCIETY

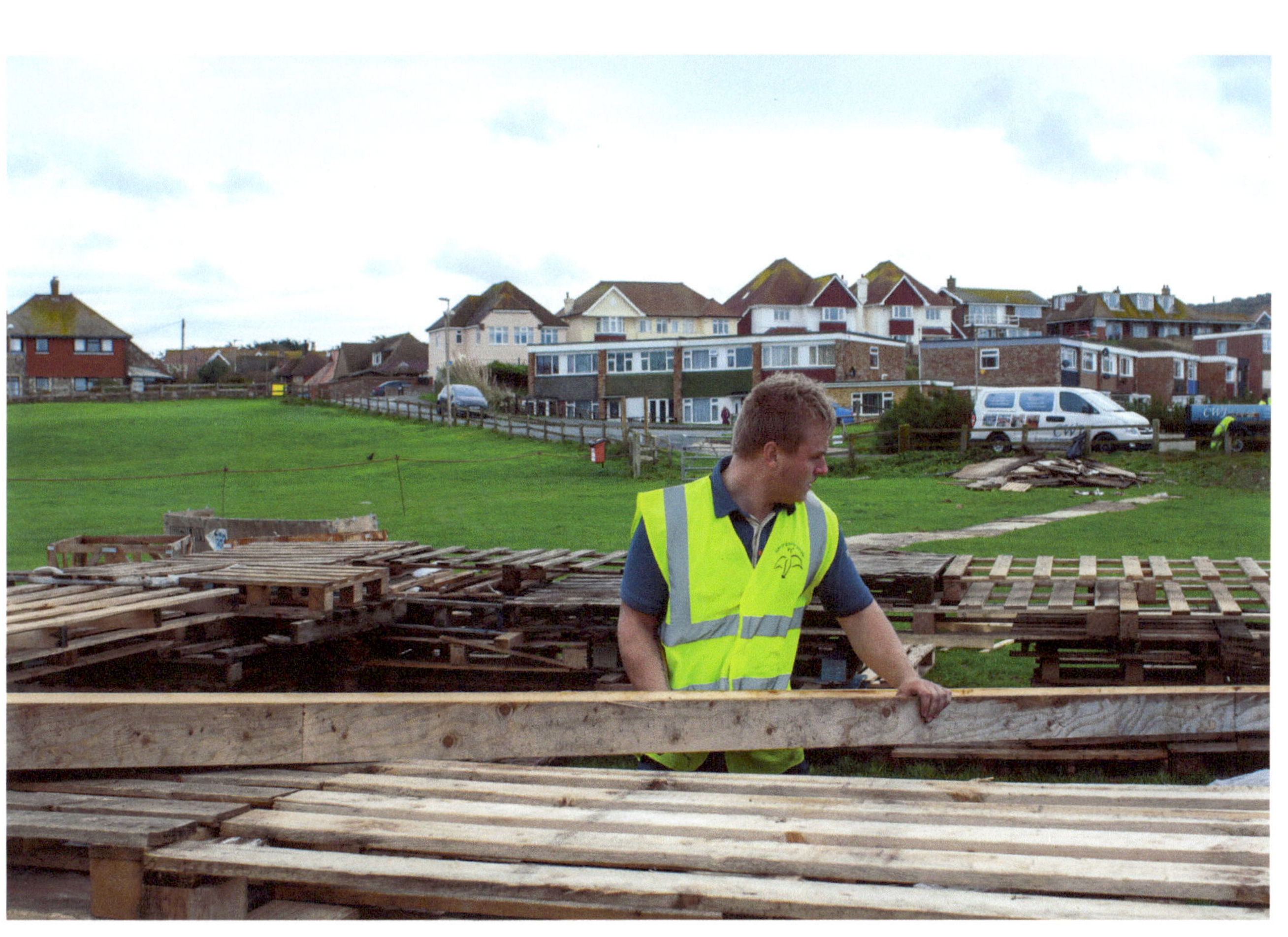

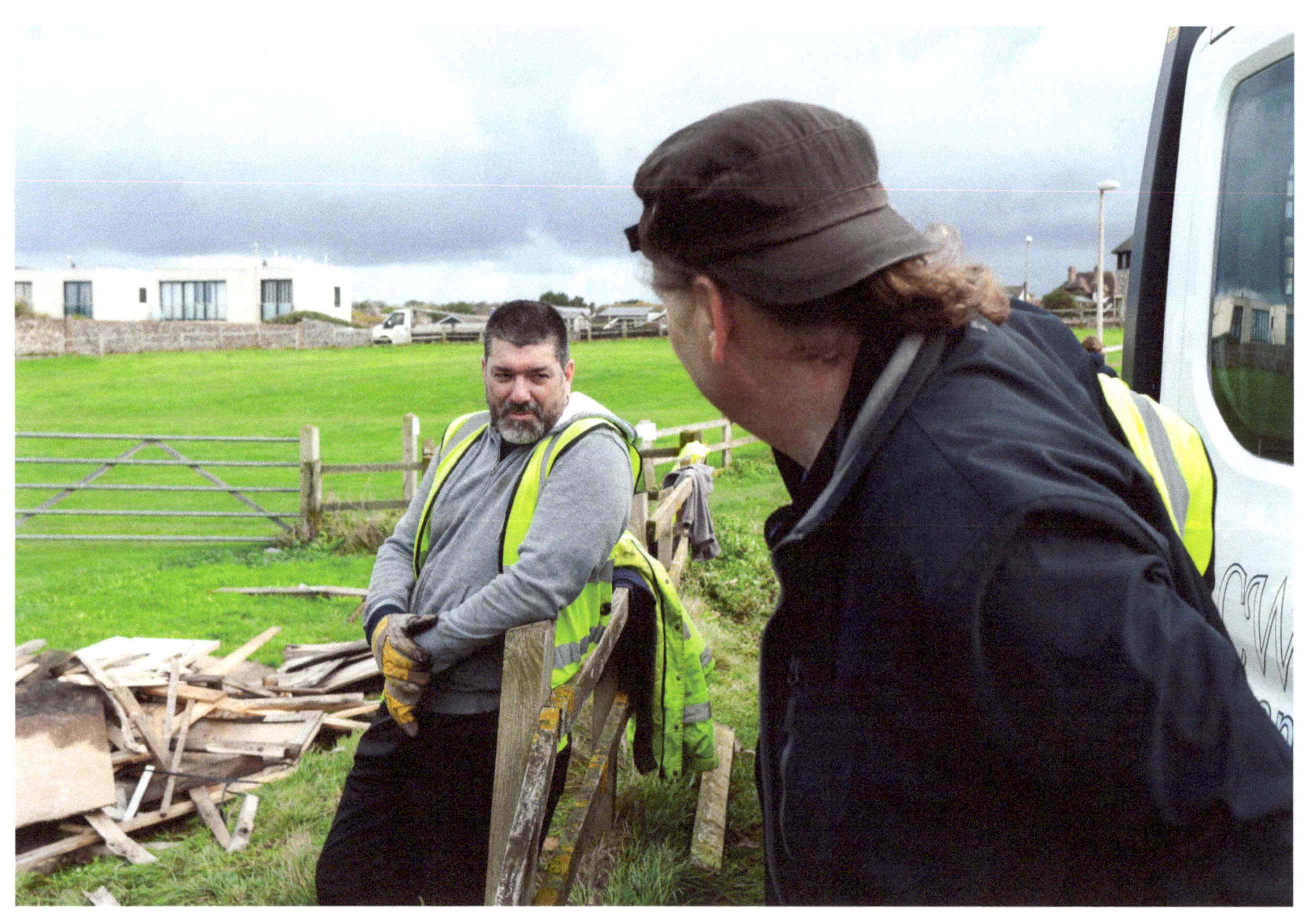

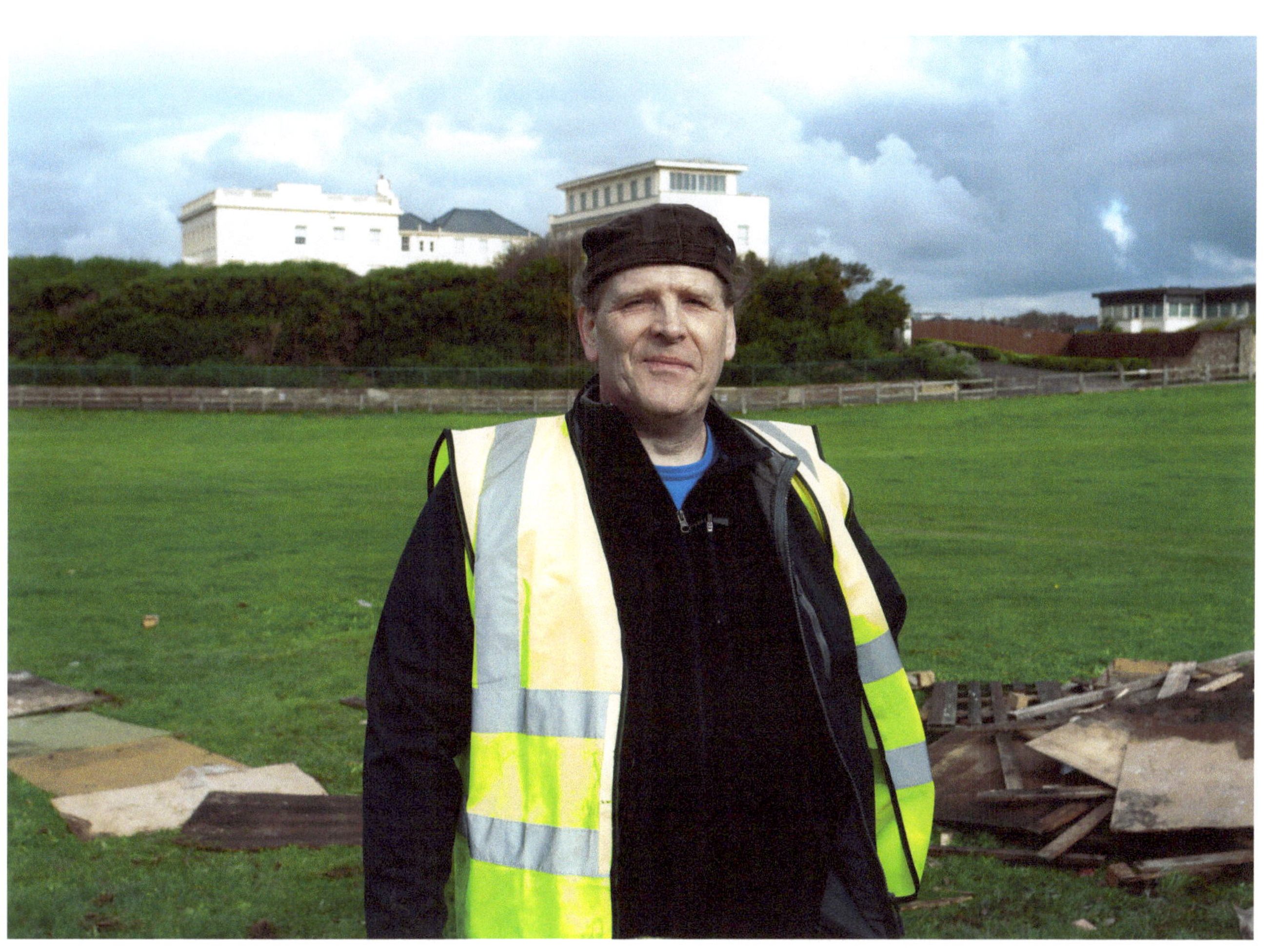

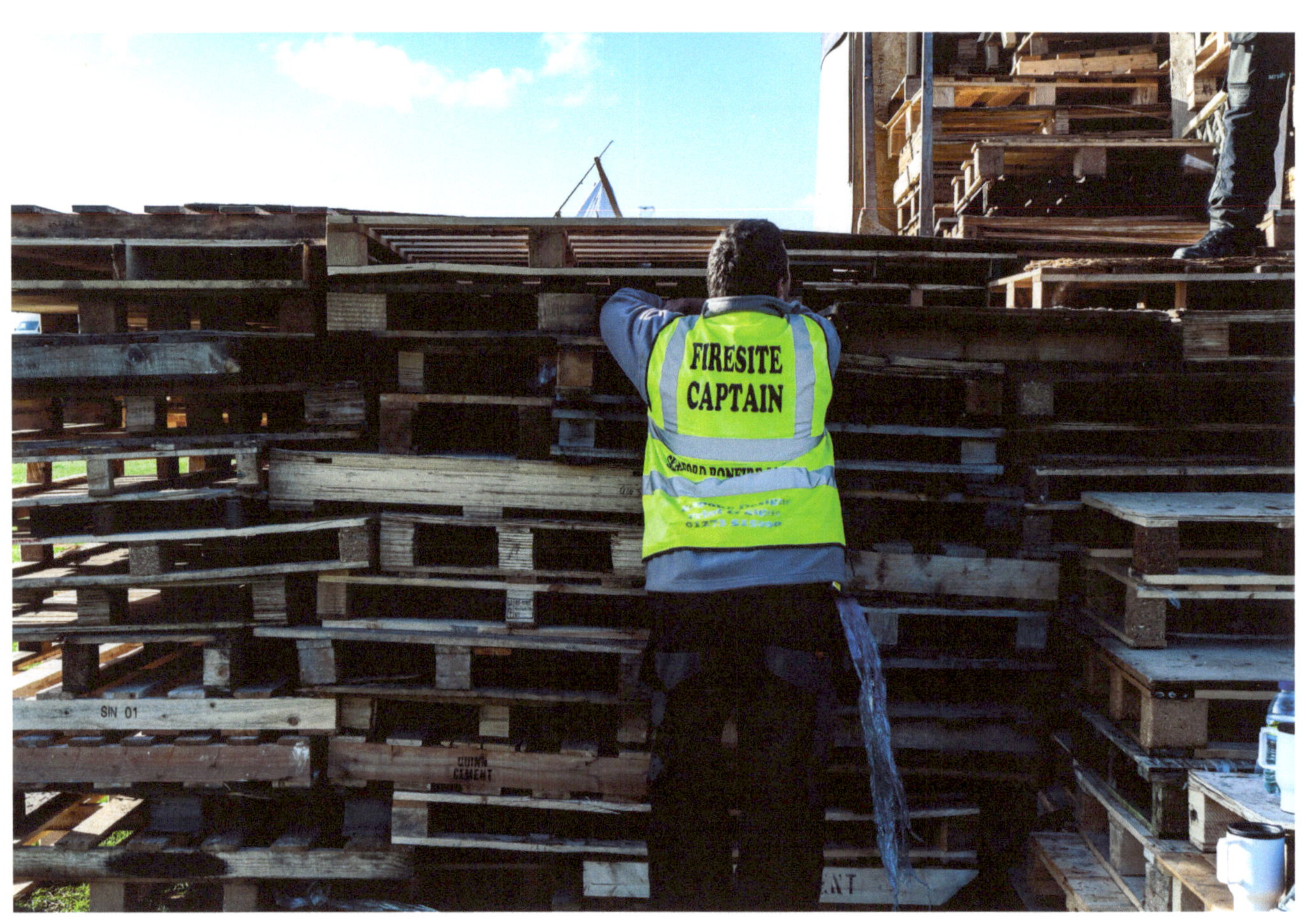

FIRESITE
CAPTAIN

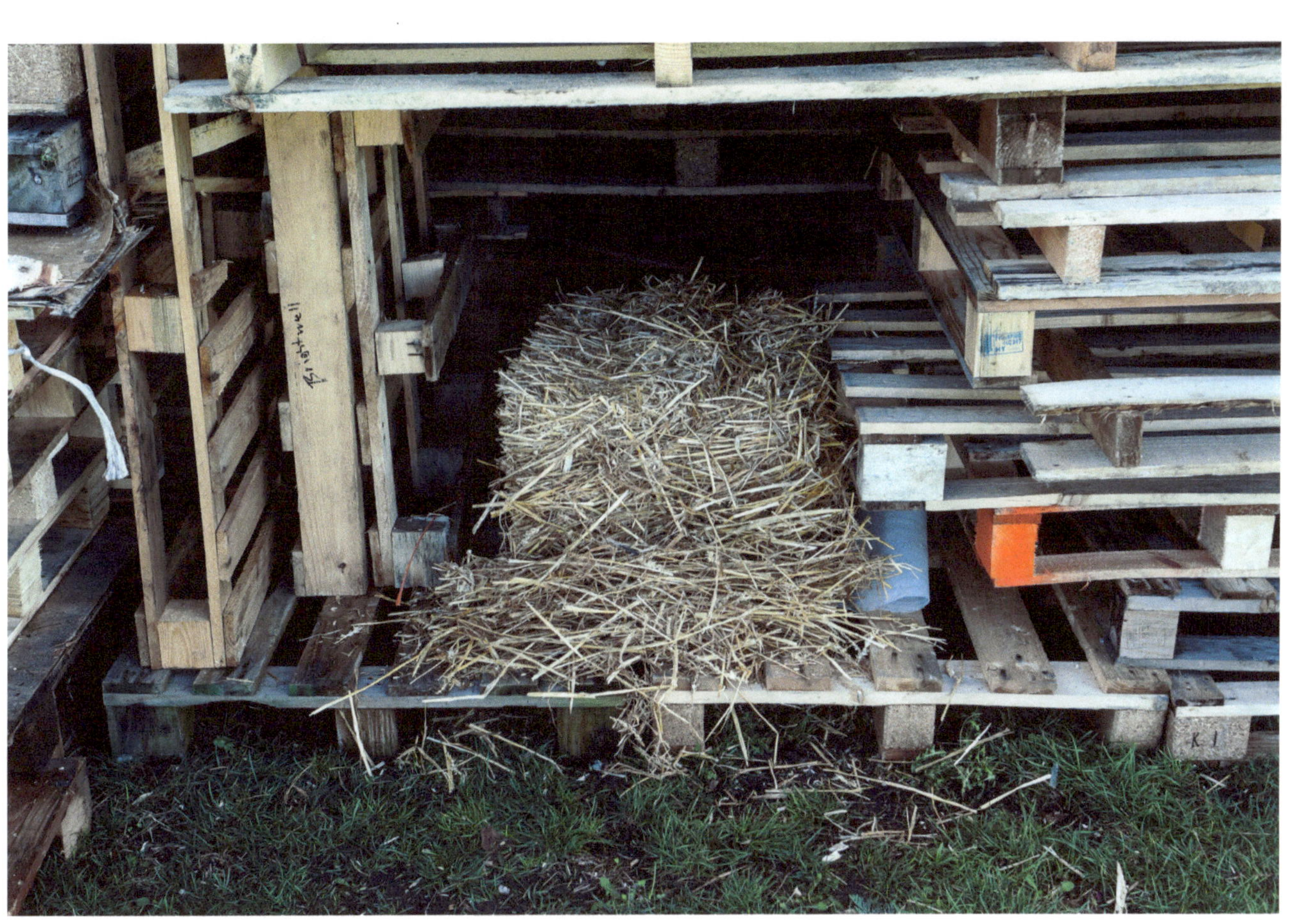

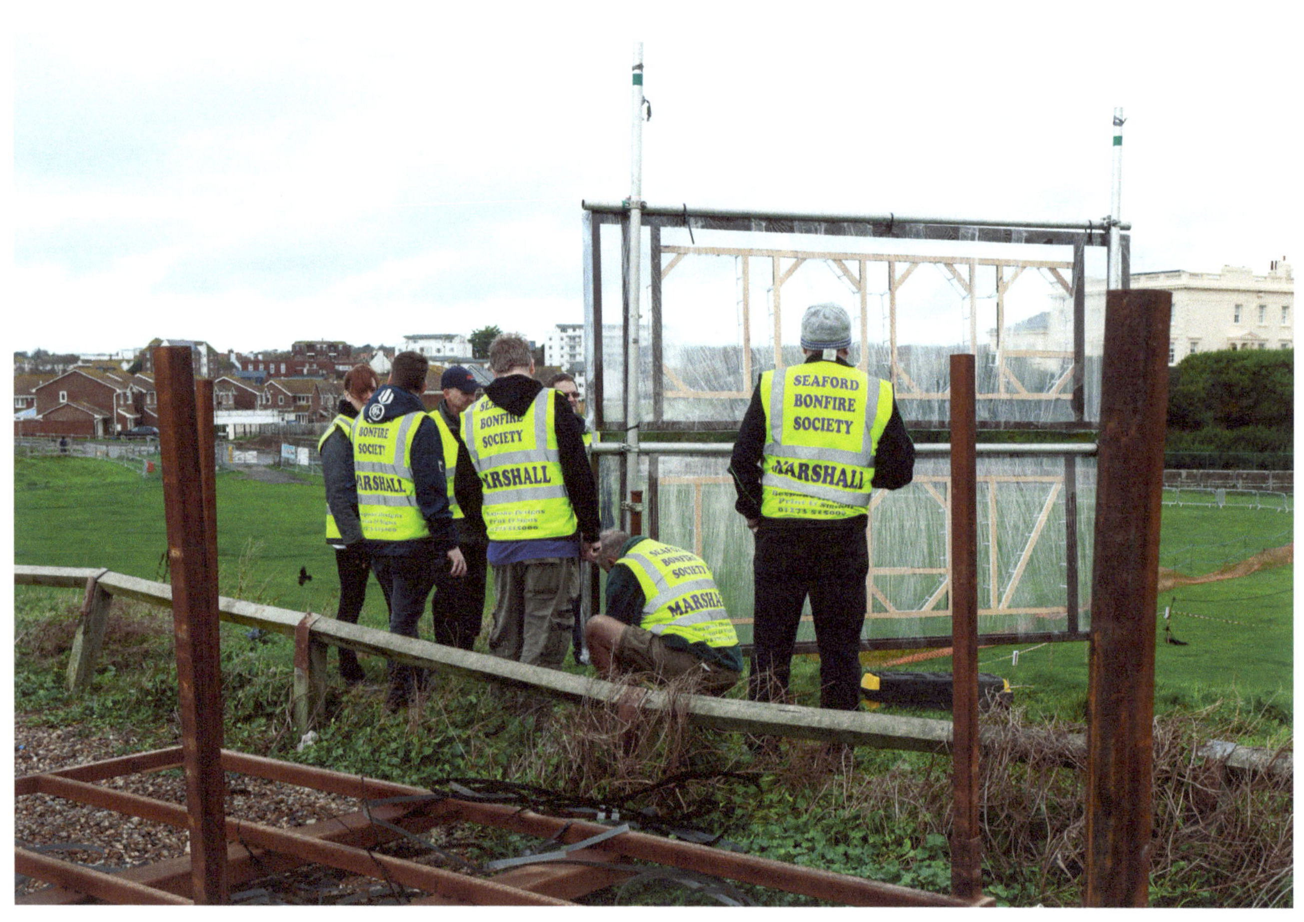

SEAFORD
BONFIRE
SOCIETY
MARSHALL

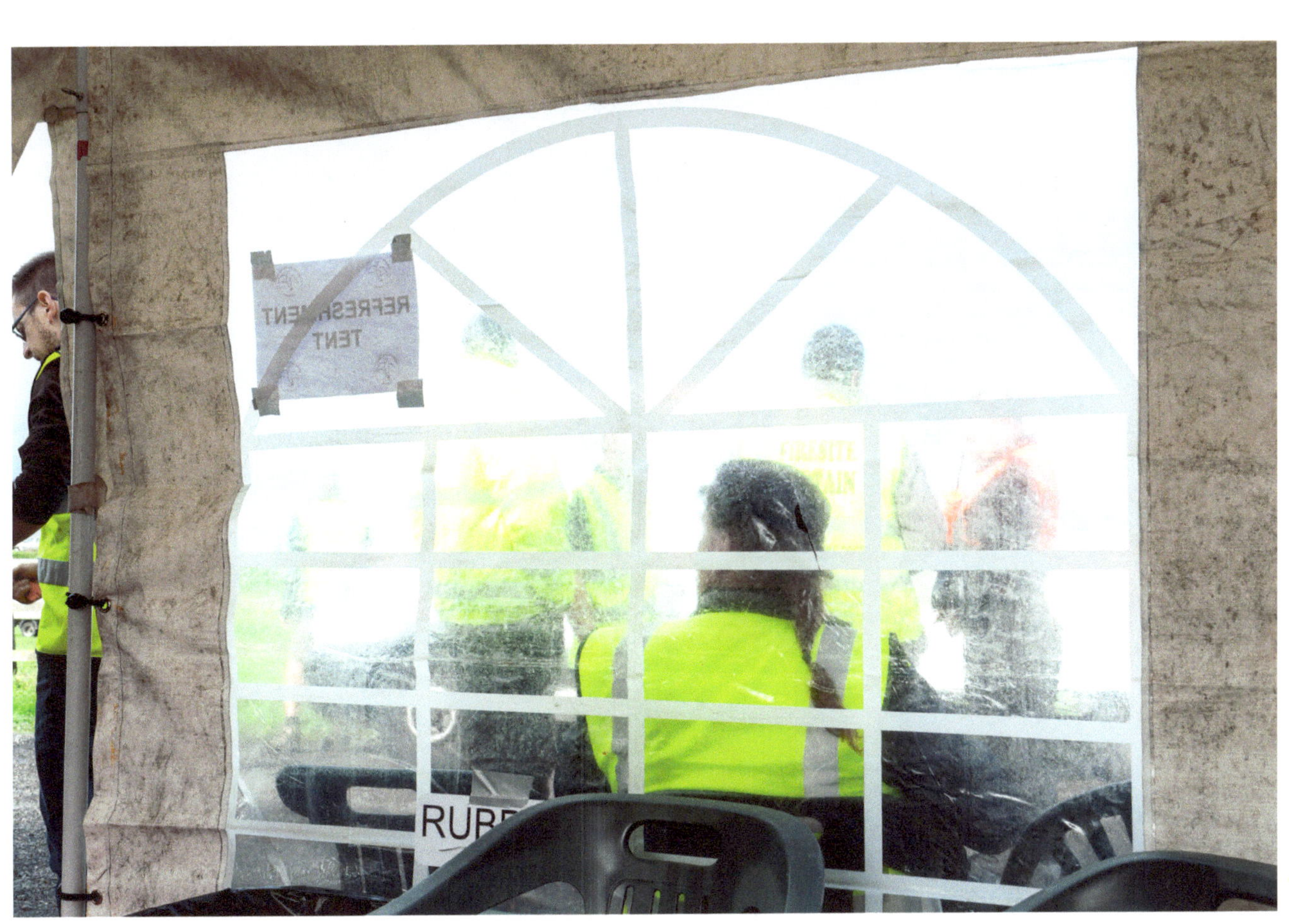
REFRESHMENT
TENT
RUBE

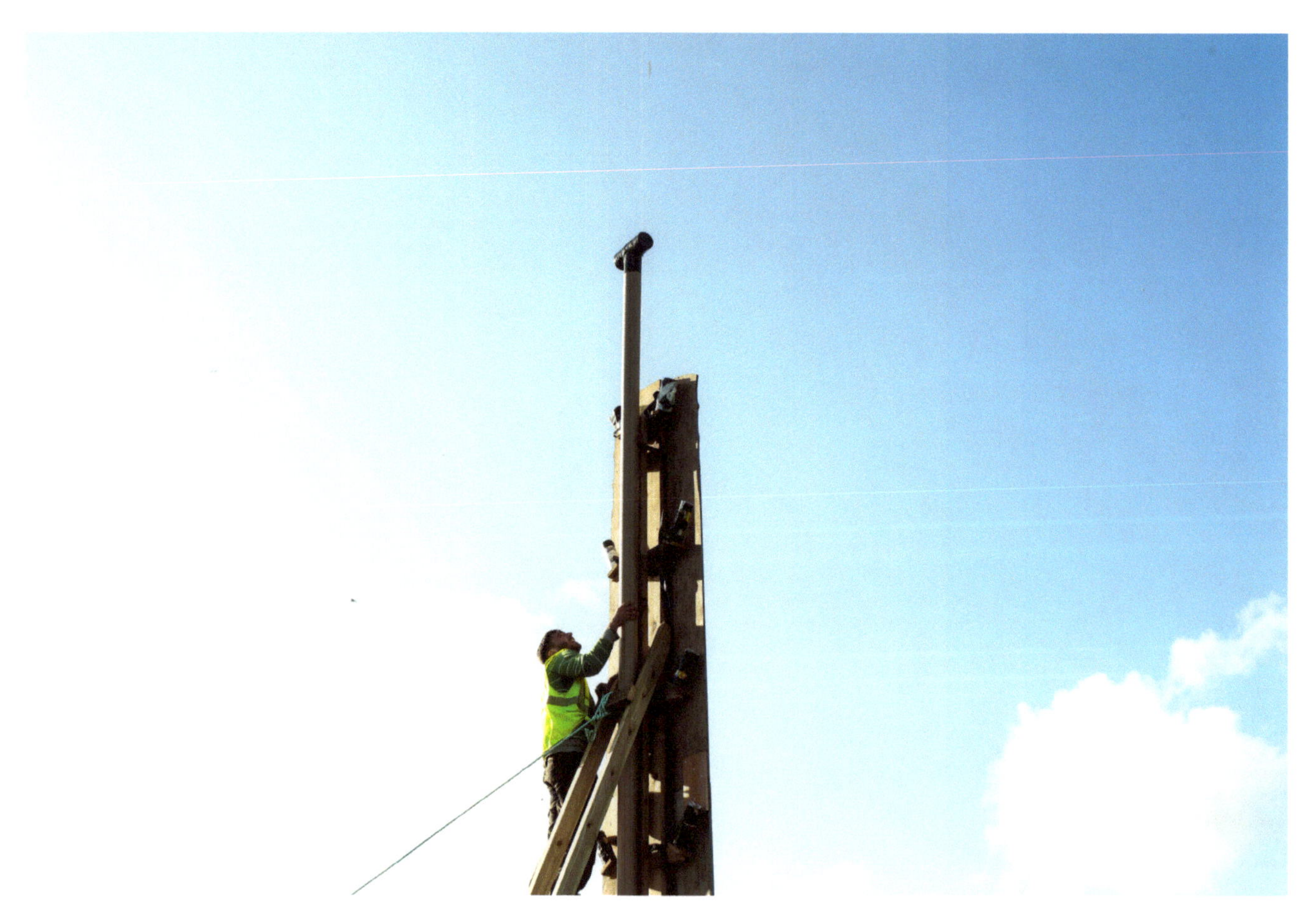

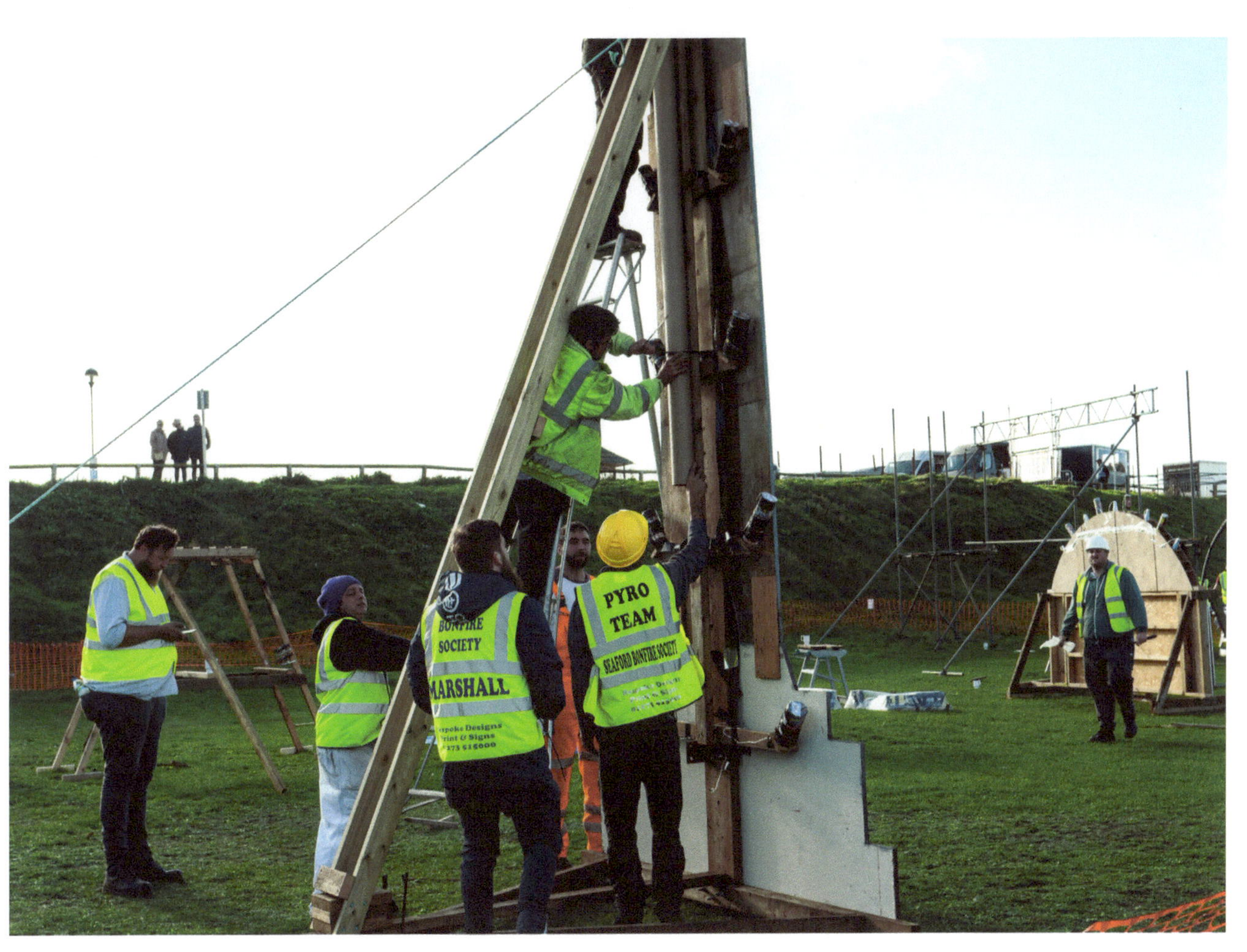

BONFIRE
SOCIETY
MARSHALL
PYRO
TEAM
SEAFORD BONFIRE SOCIETY

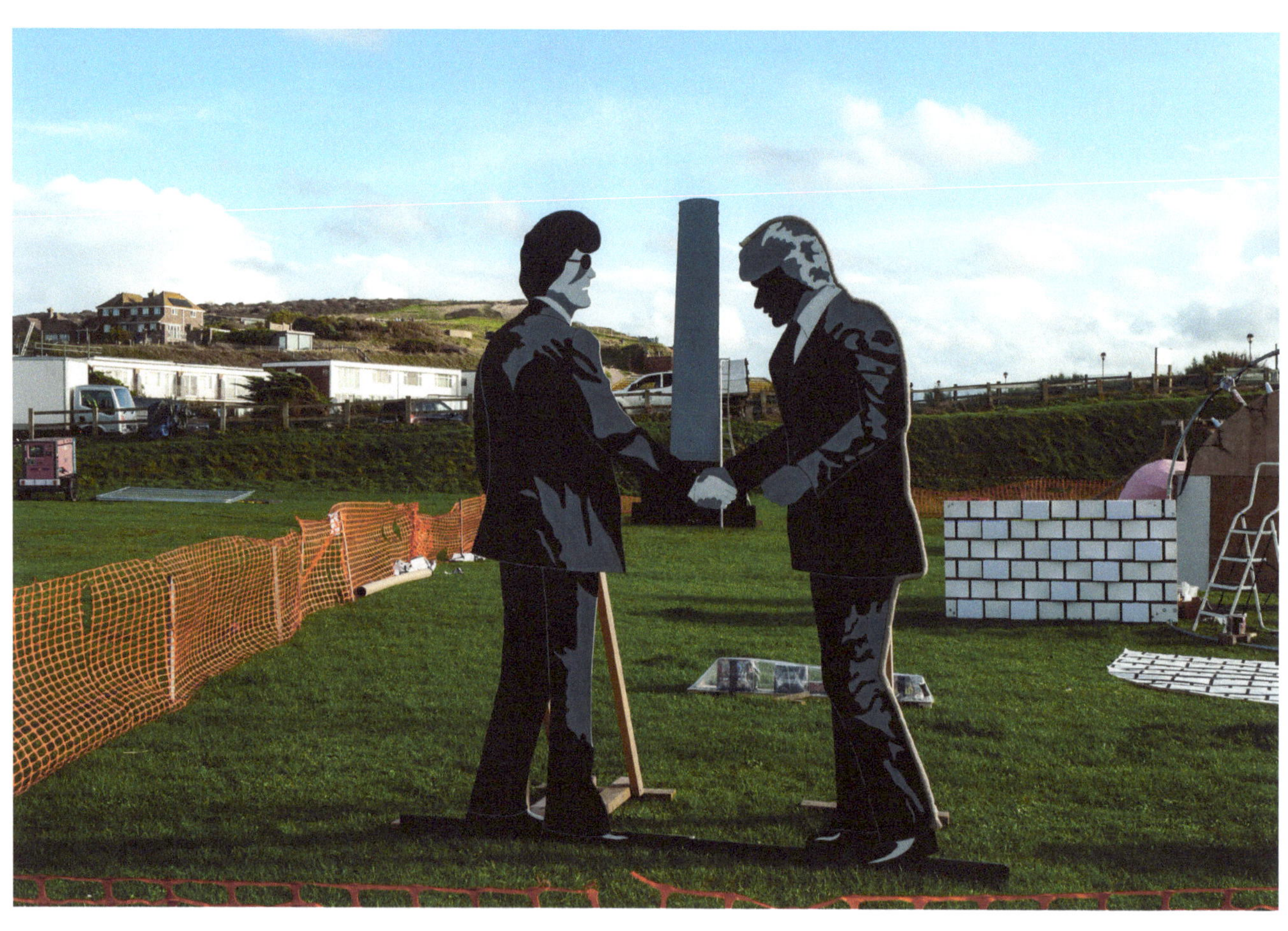

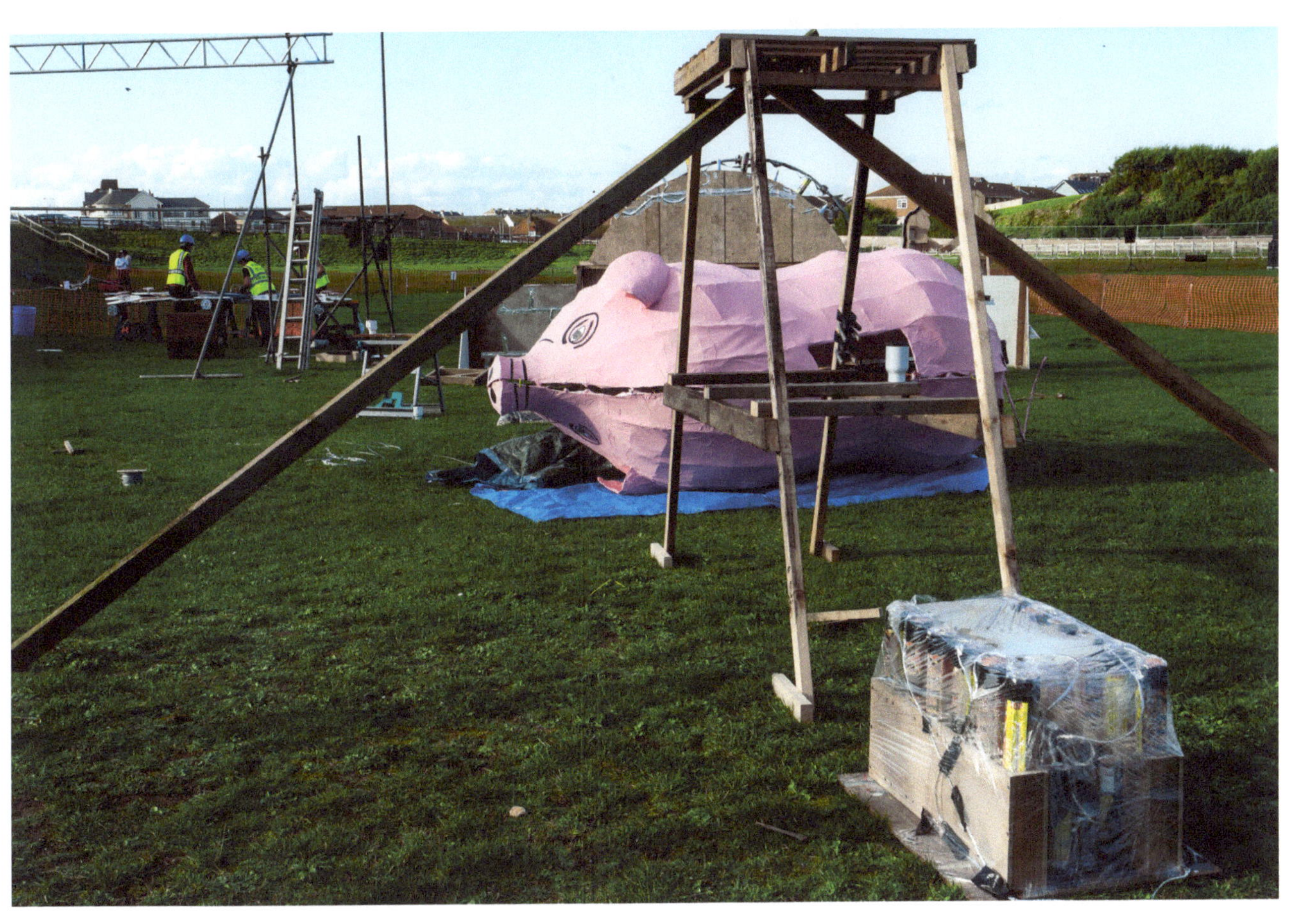

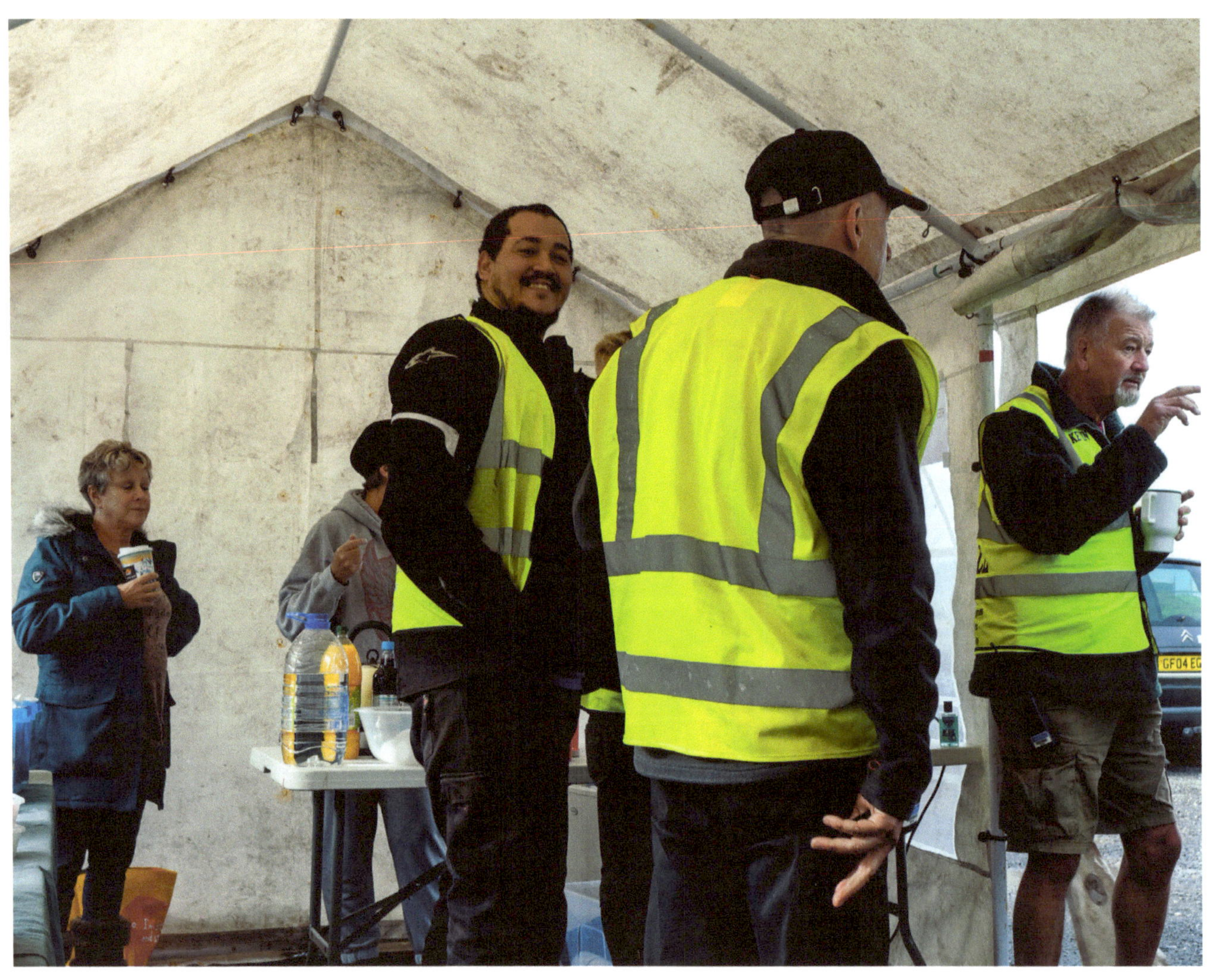

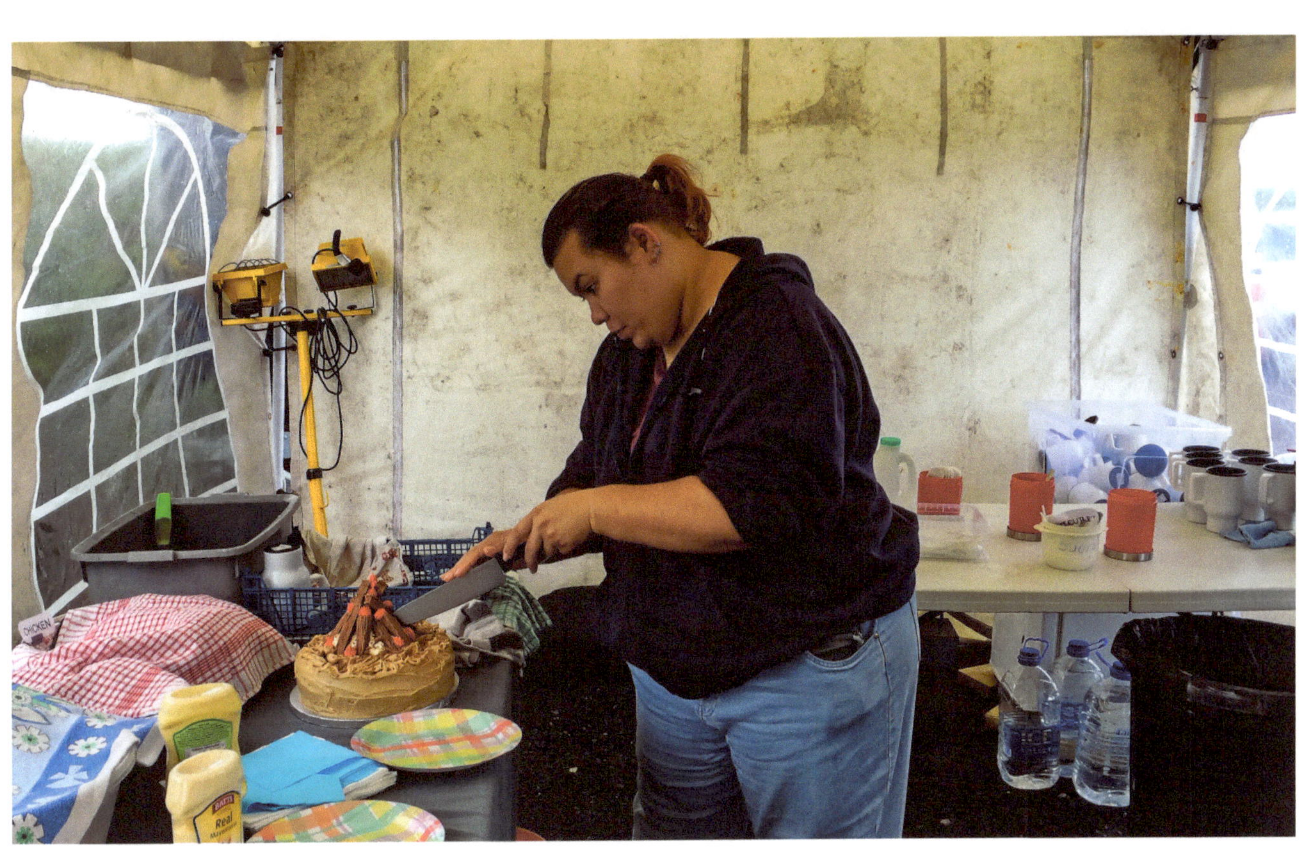

People

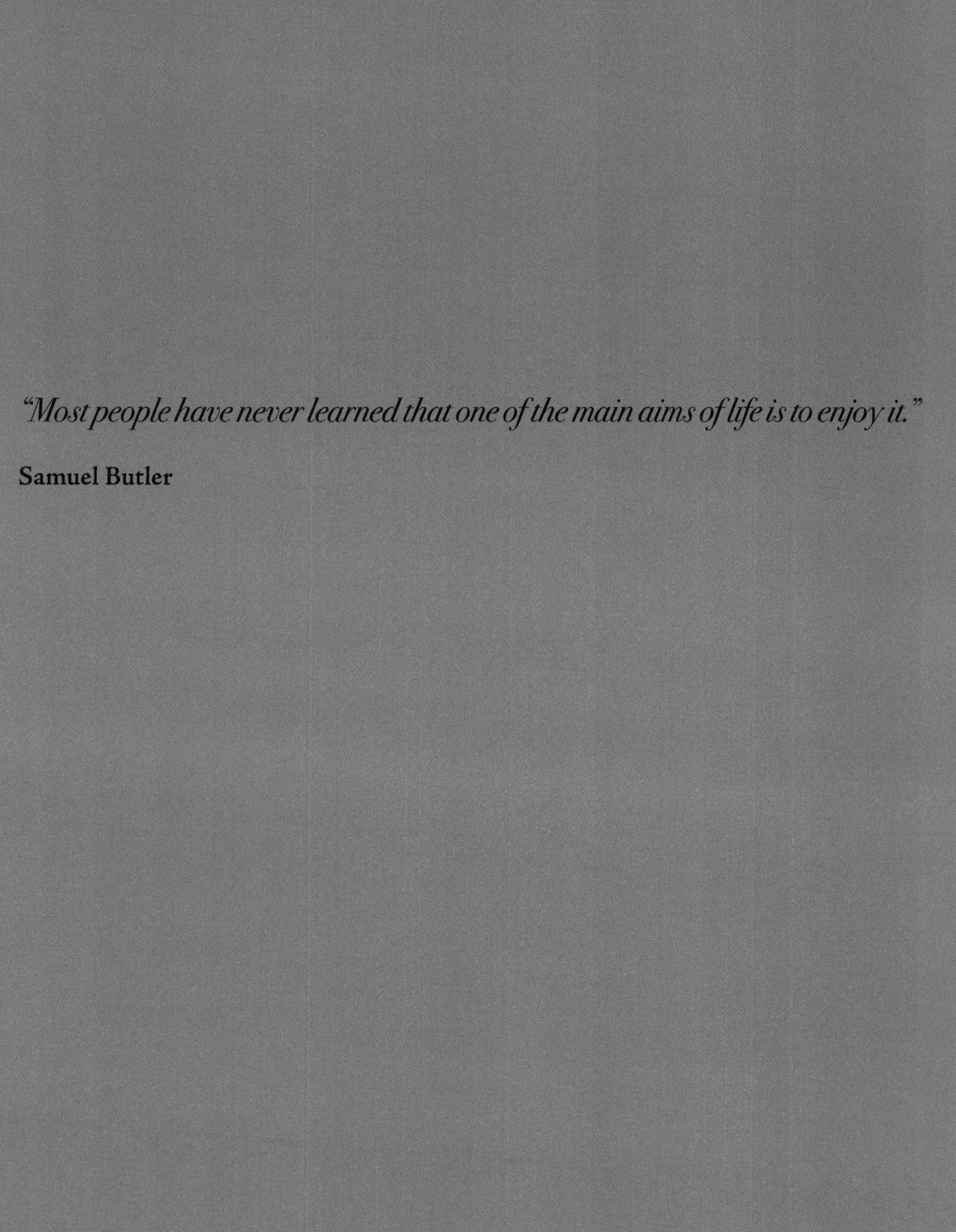

"Most people have never learned that one of the main aims of life is to enjoy it."

Samuel Butler

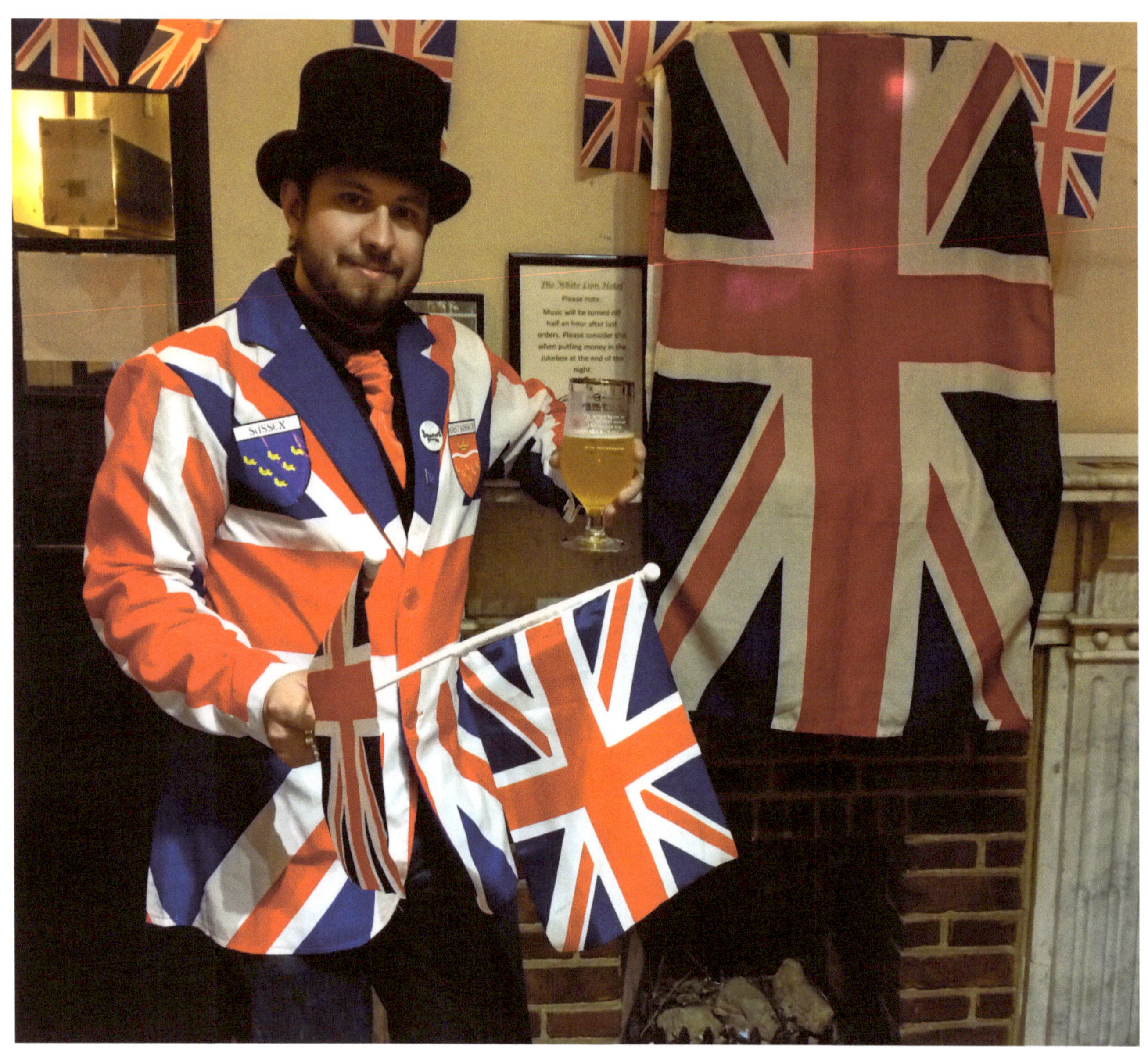

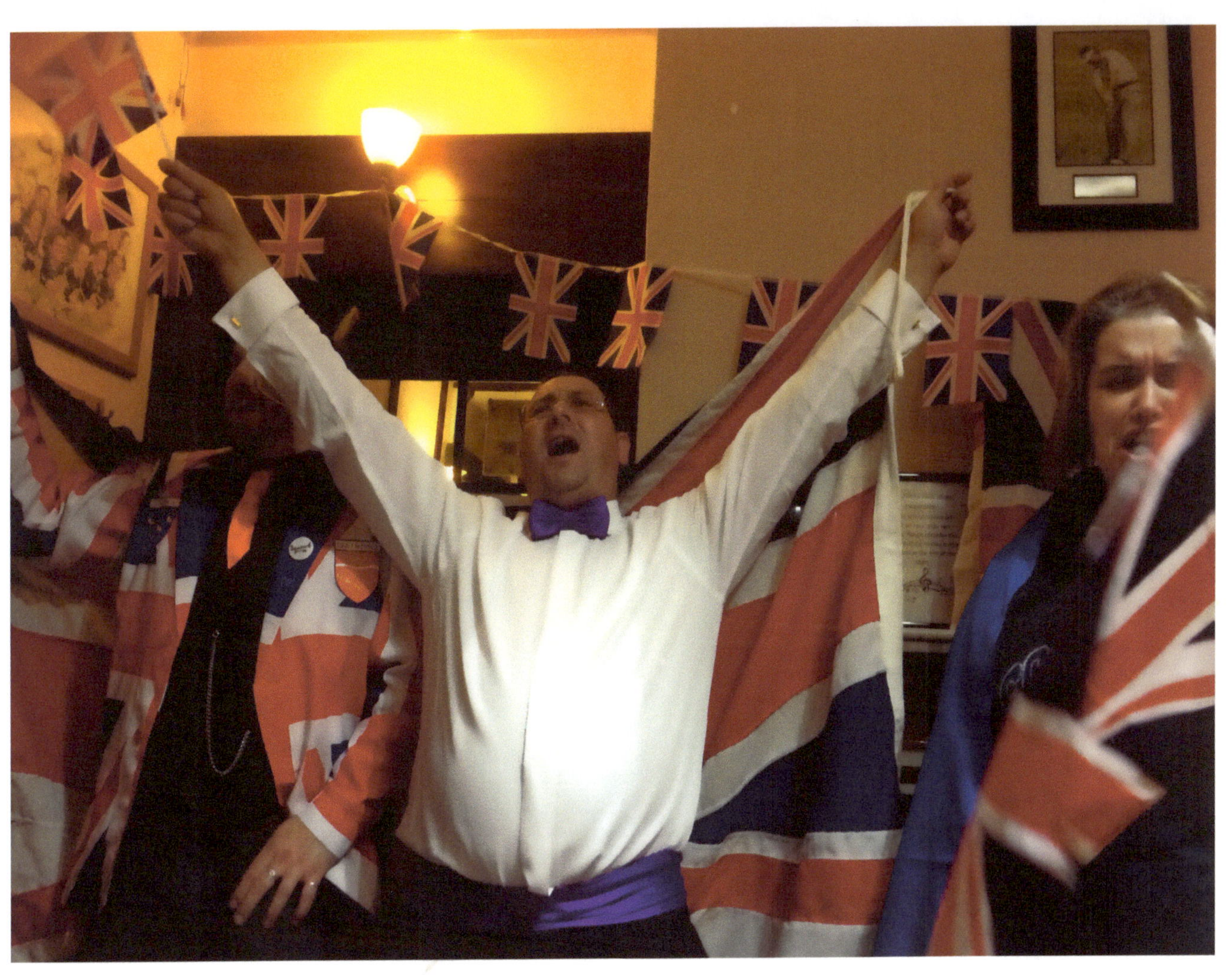

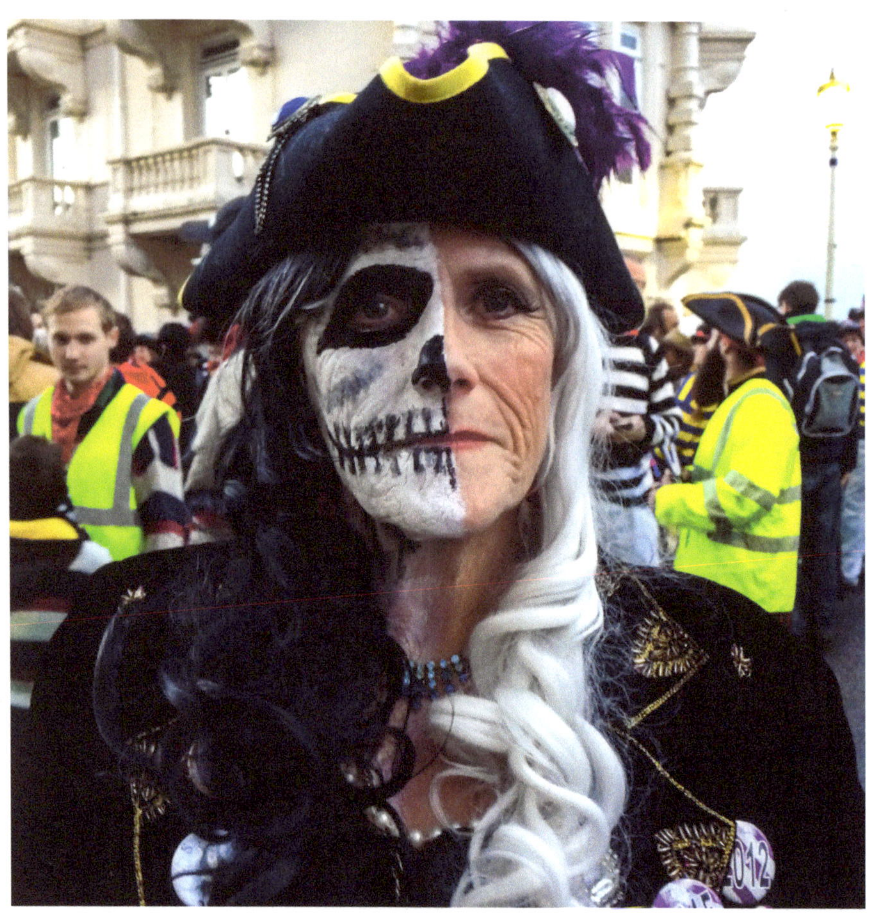

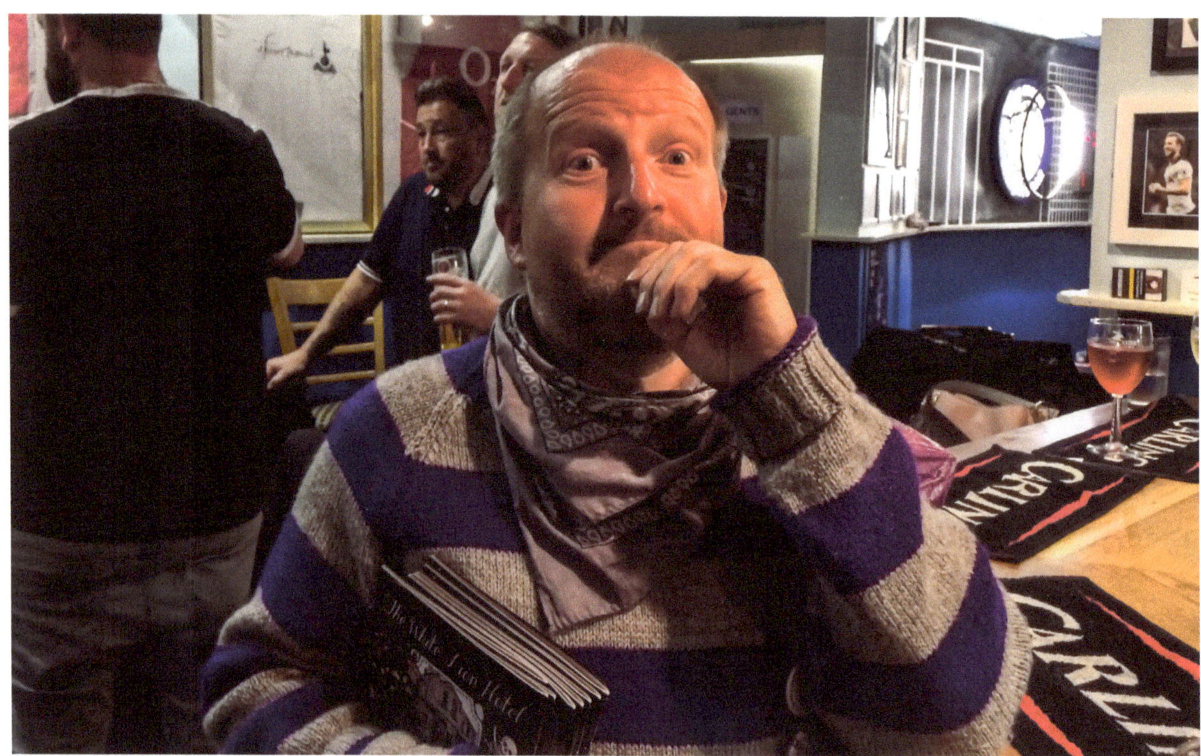

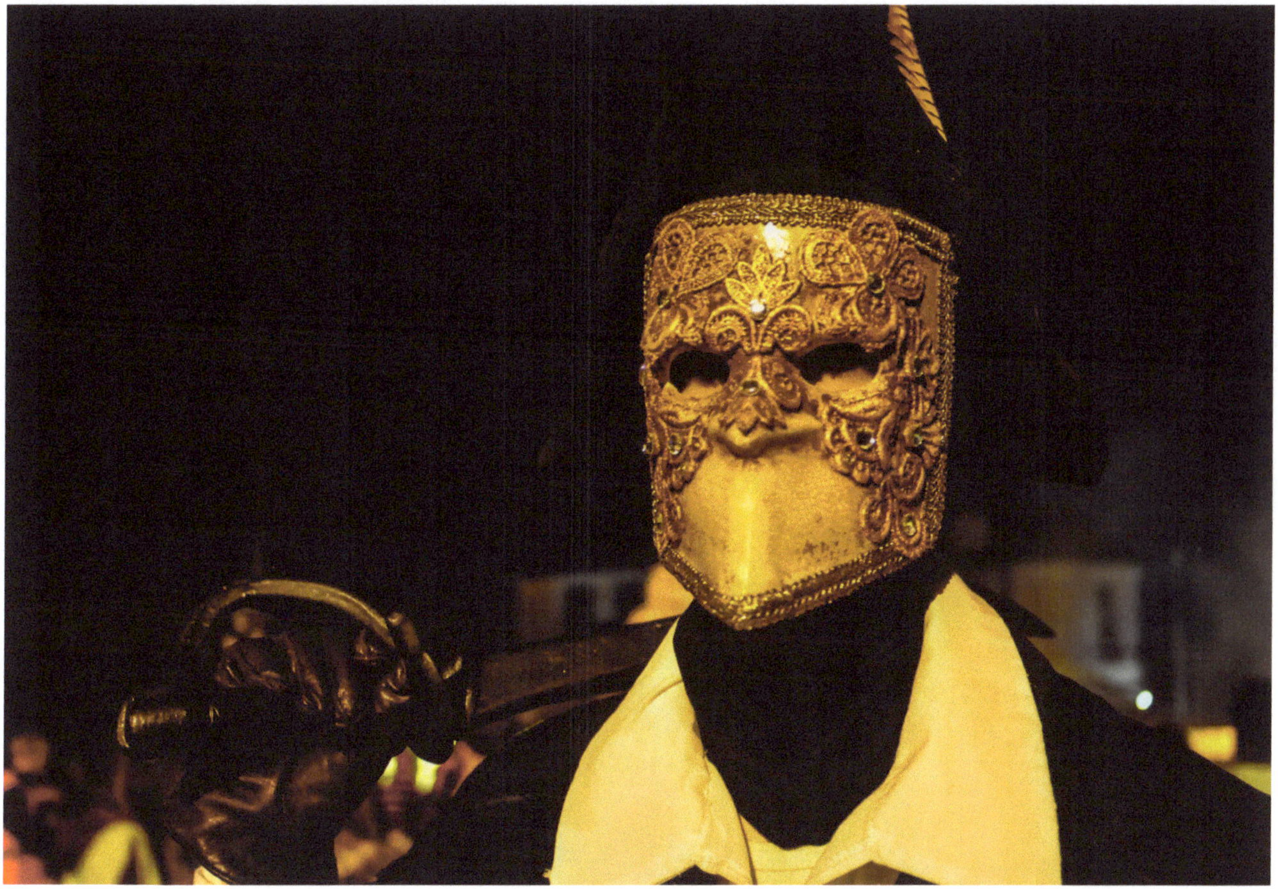

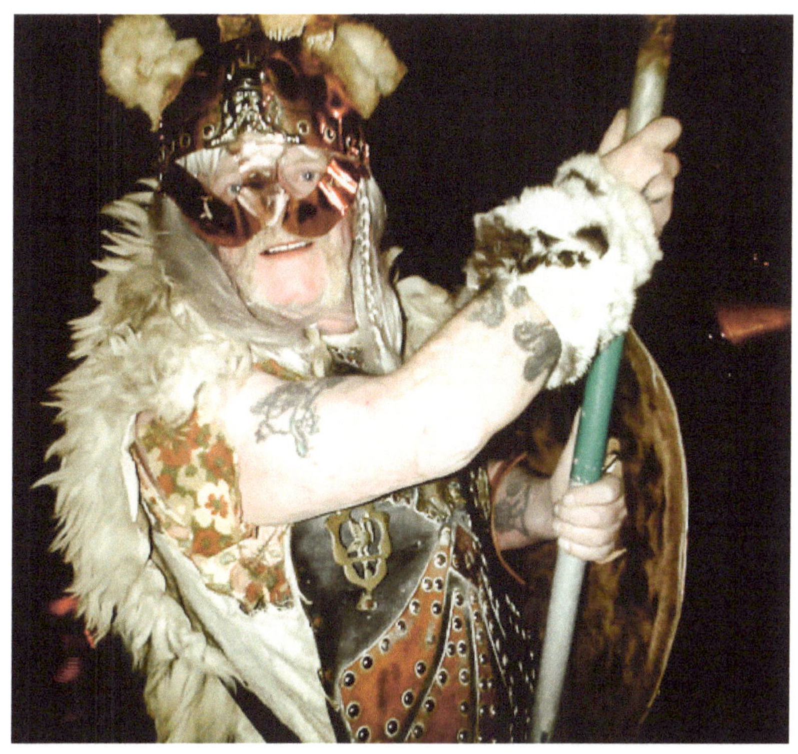

Parade

The Bonfire Prayer

Remember, remember the Fifth of November
The Gunpowder Treason and plot,
I see no reason why Gunpowder Treason
Should ever be forgot.
Guy Fawkes, Guy Fawkes 'twas his intent
To blow up the King and the Parliament,
Three score barrels of powder below
Poor old England to overthrow.
By God's providence he was catch'd
With a dark lantern and burning match,
Holler boys, holler boys, ring bells ring
Holler boys, holler boys, God Save the King!
A penny loaf to feed the Pope
A farthing o'cheese to choke him,
A pint of beer to rinse it down
A faggot of sticks to burn him.
Burn him in a tub of tar
Burn him like a blazing star,
Burn his body from his head
Then we'll say old Pope is dead.
Hip Hip Hoorah!
Hip Hip Hoorah!
Hip Hip Hoorah!

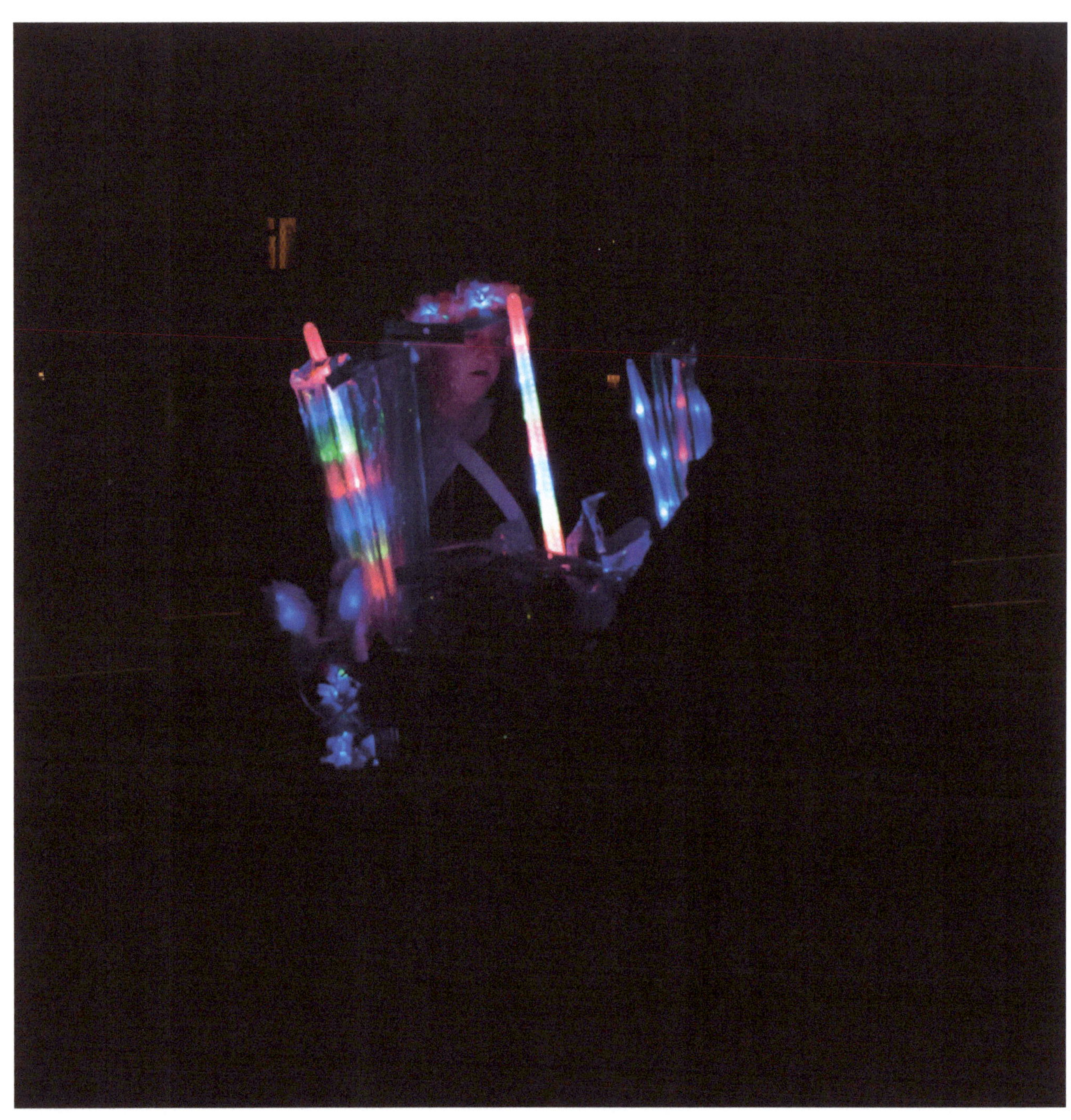

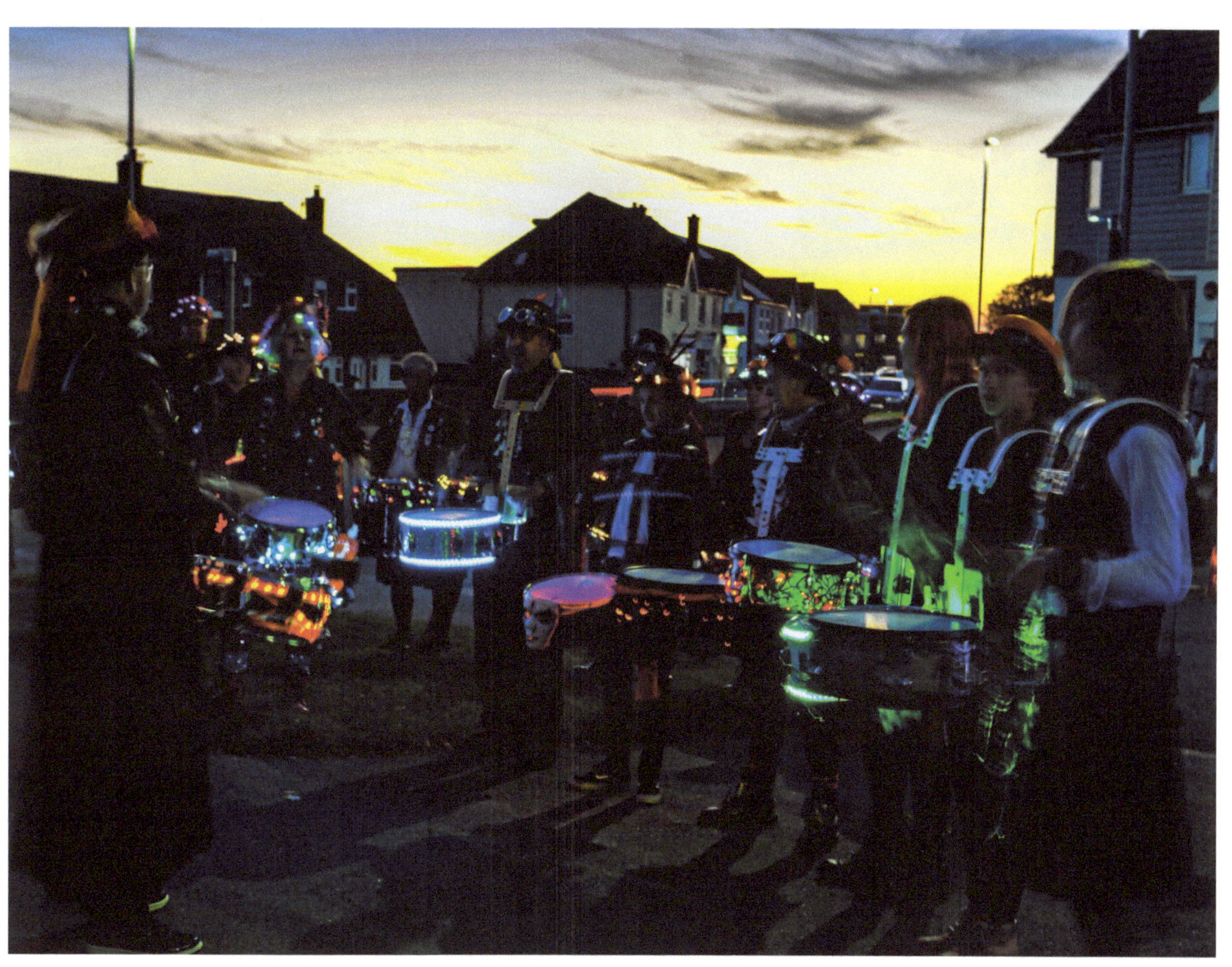

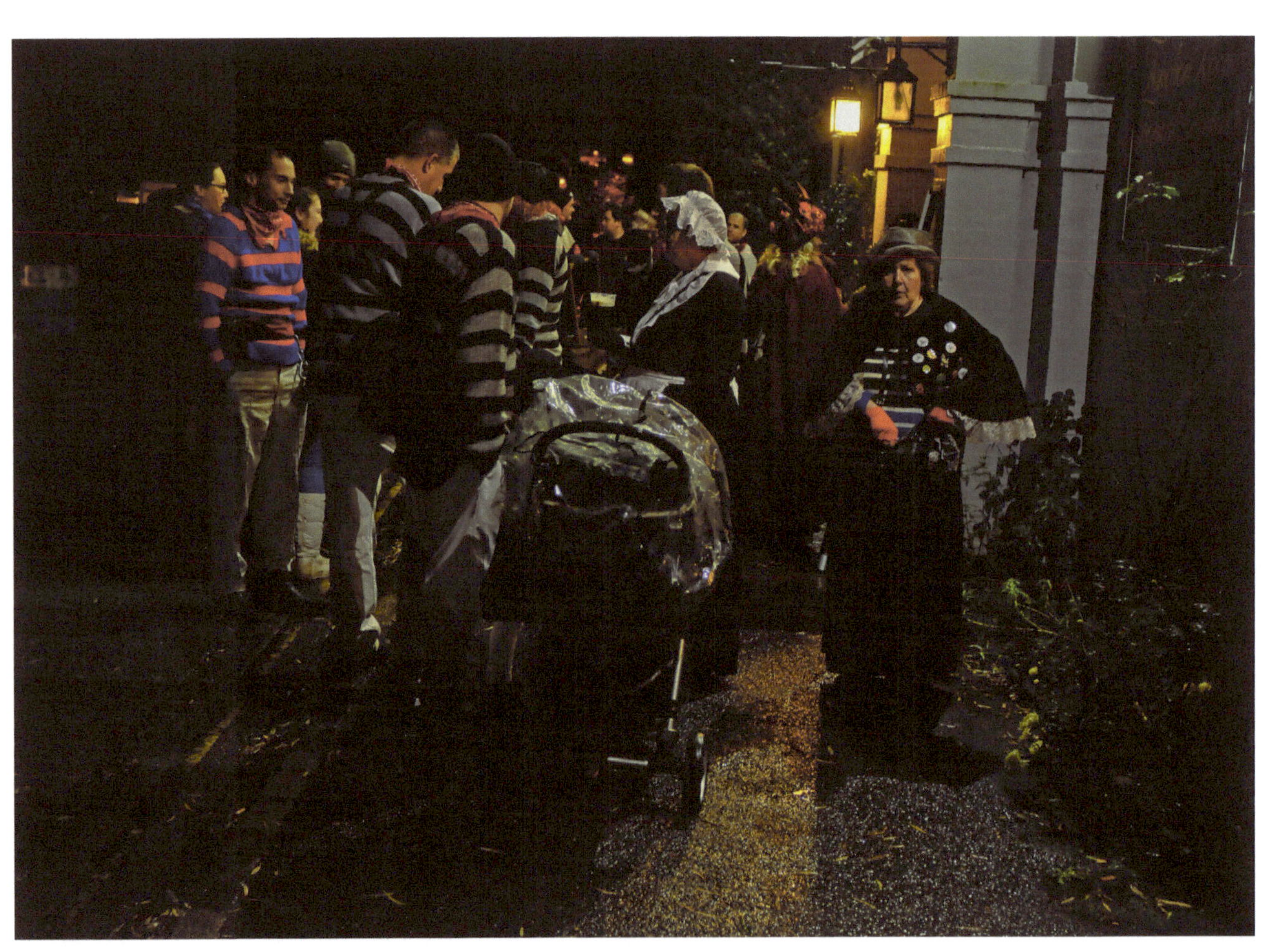

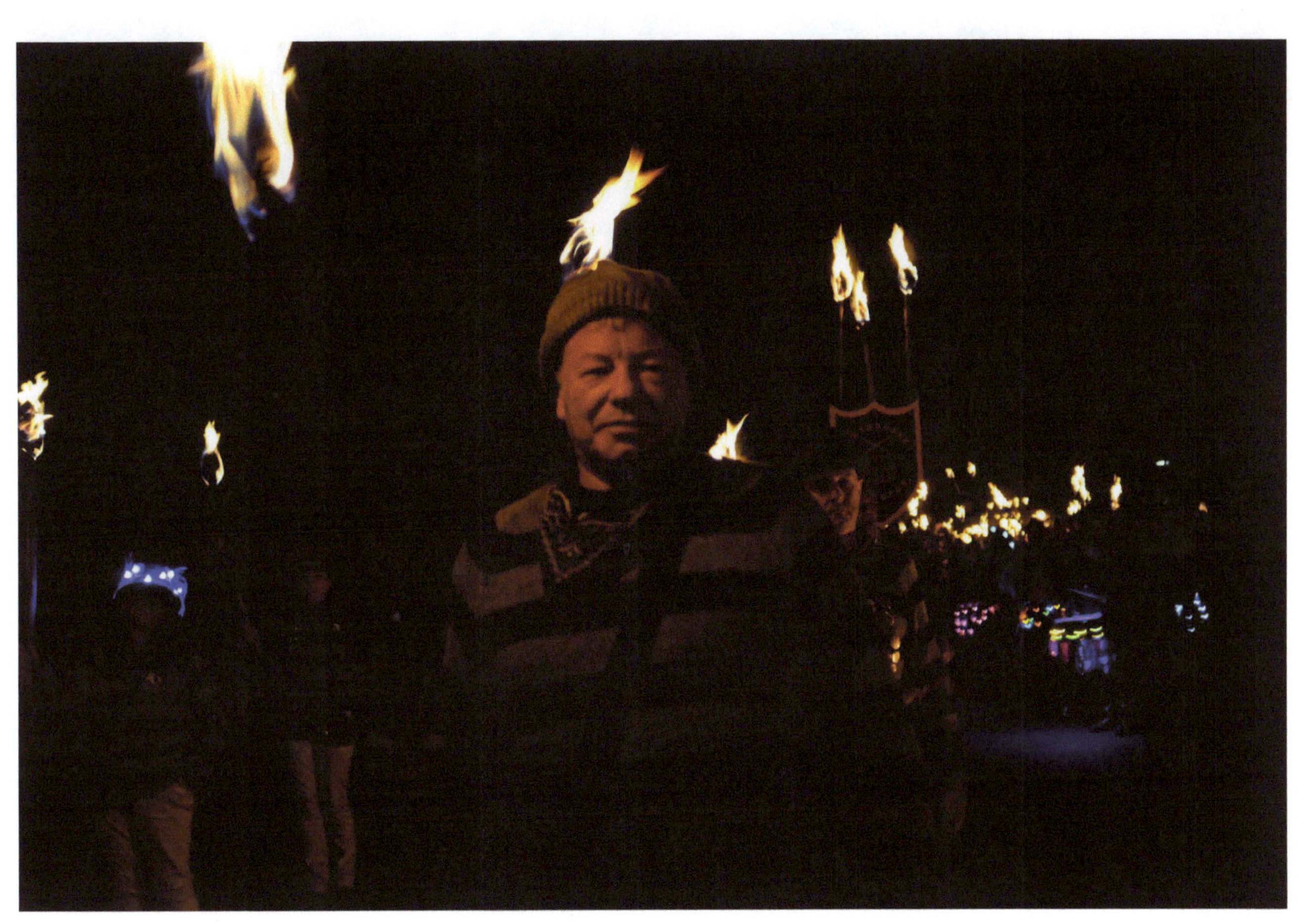

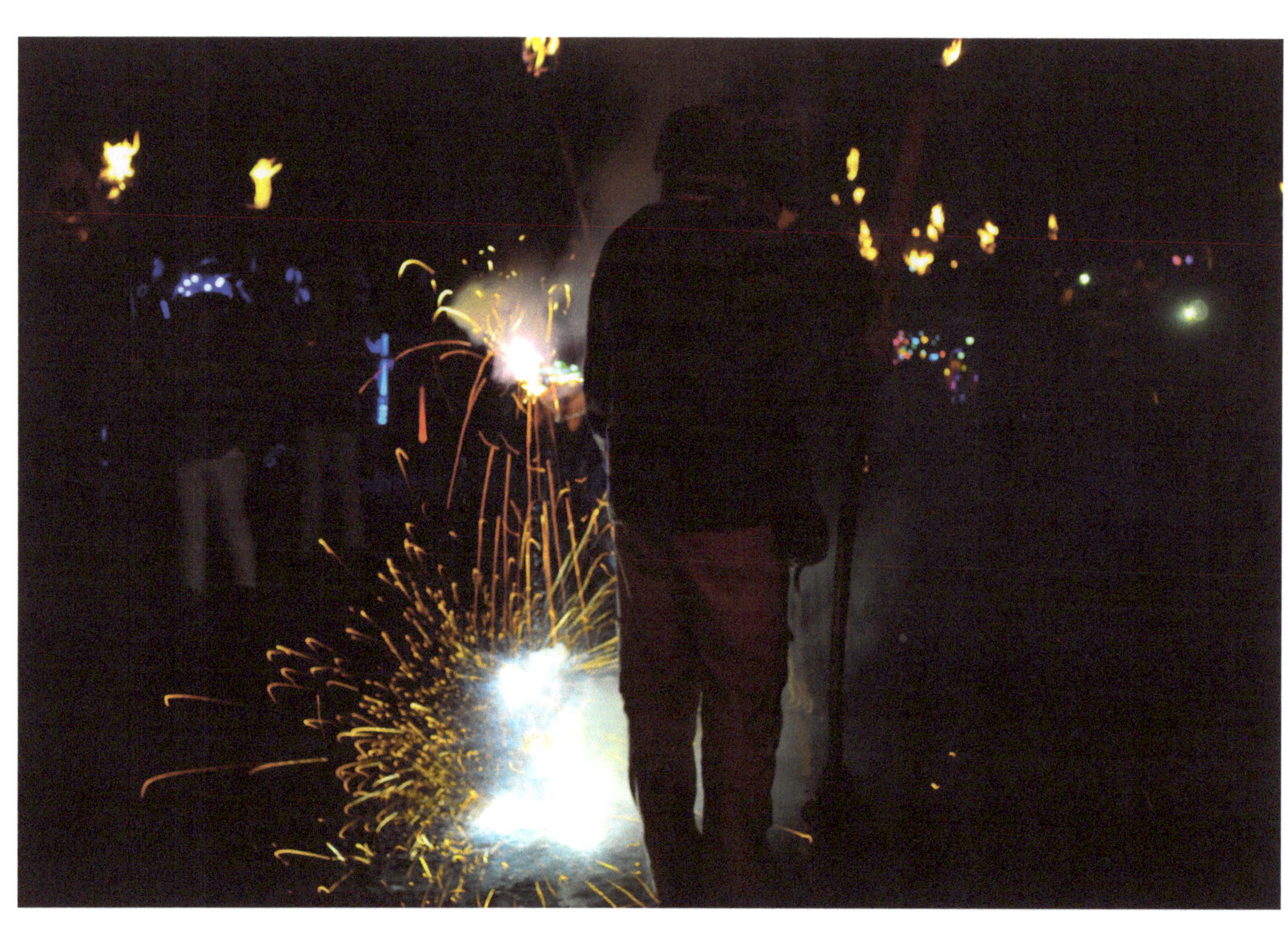

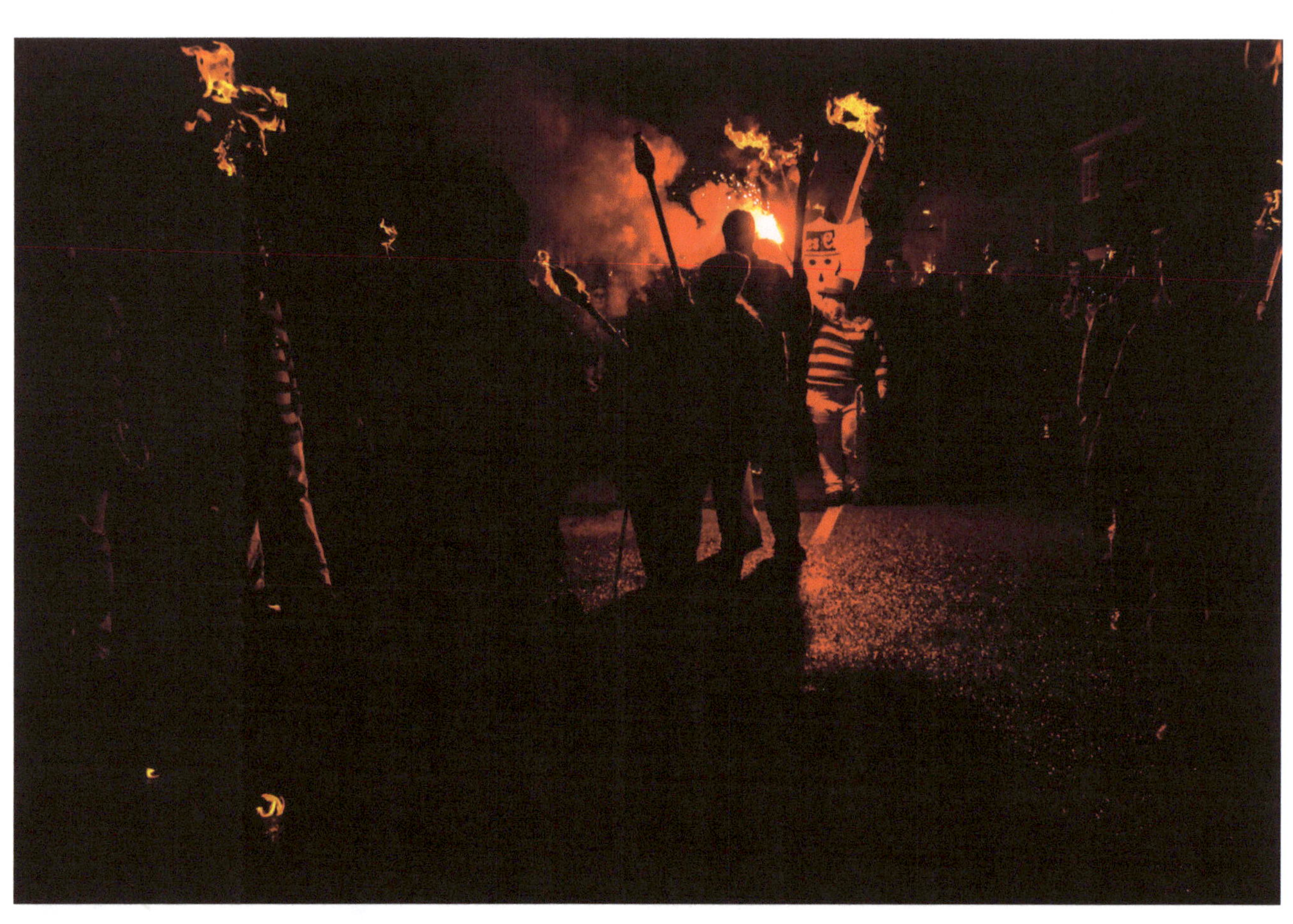

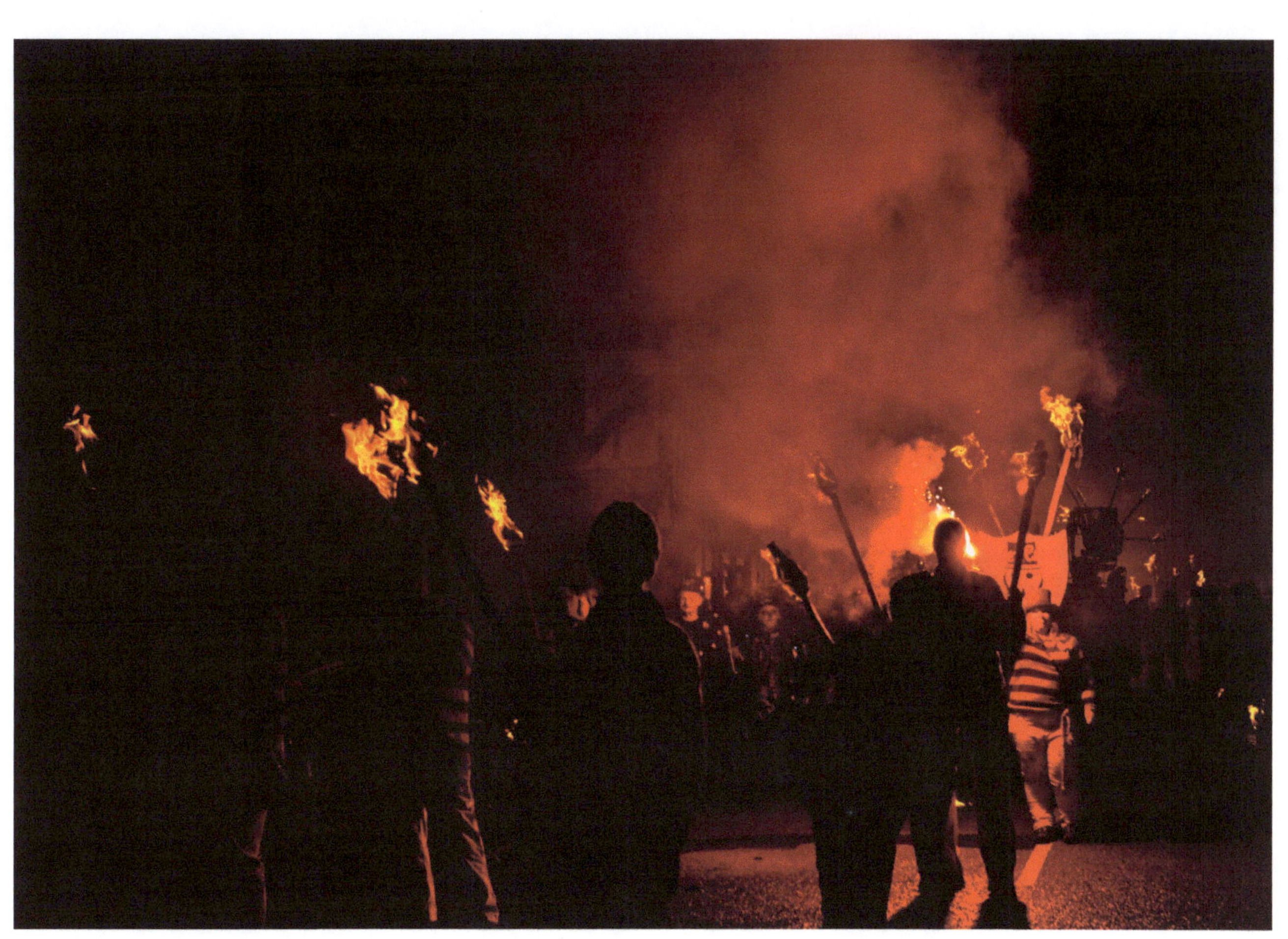

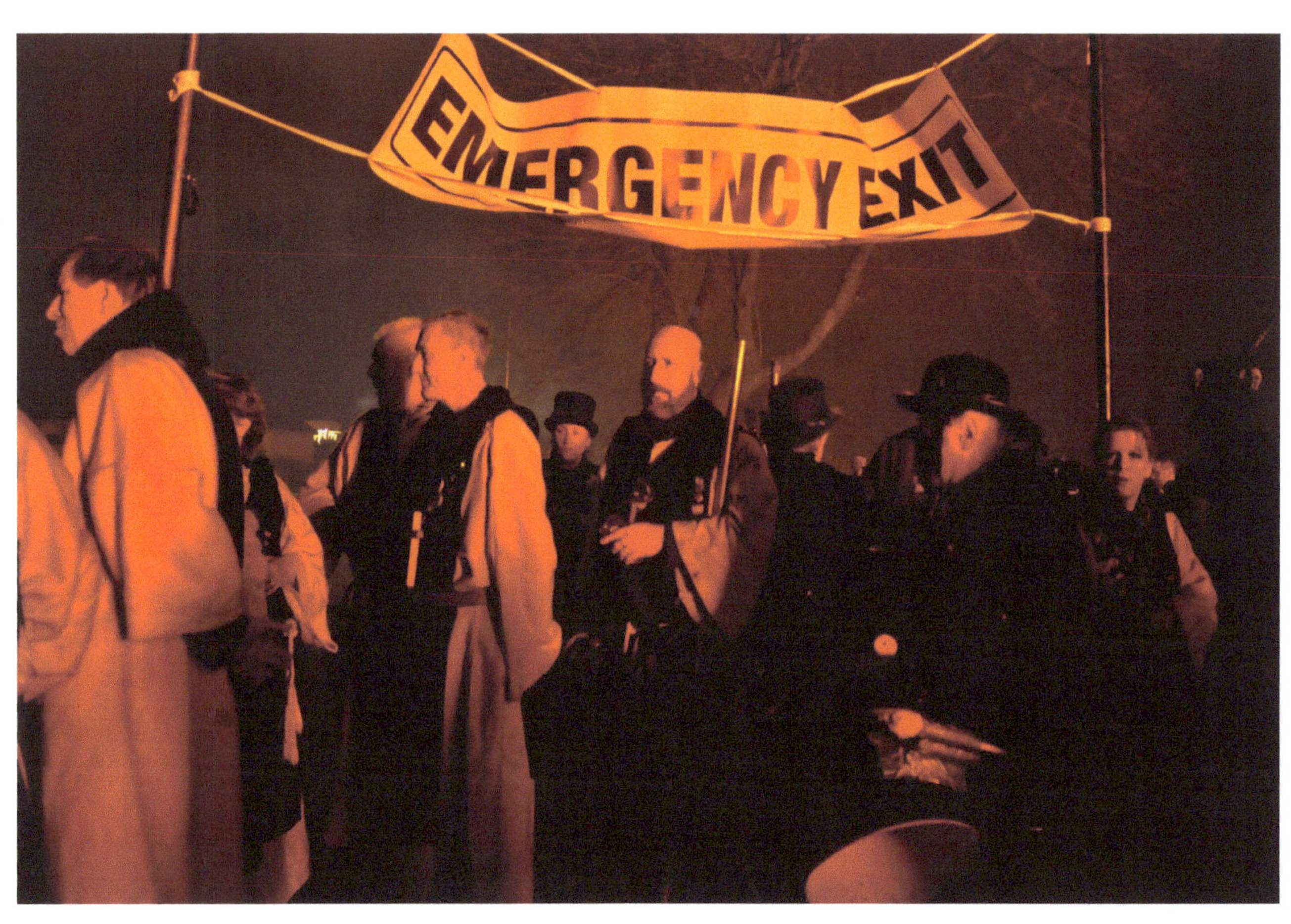
EMERGENCY EXIT

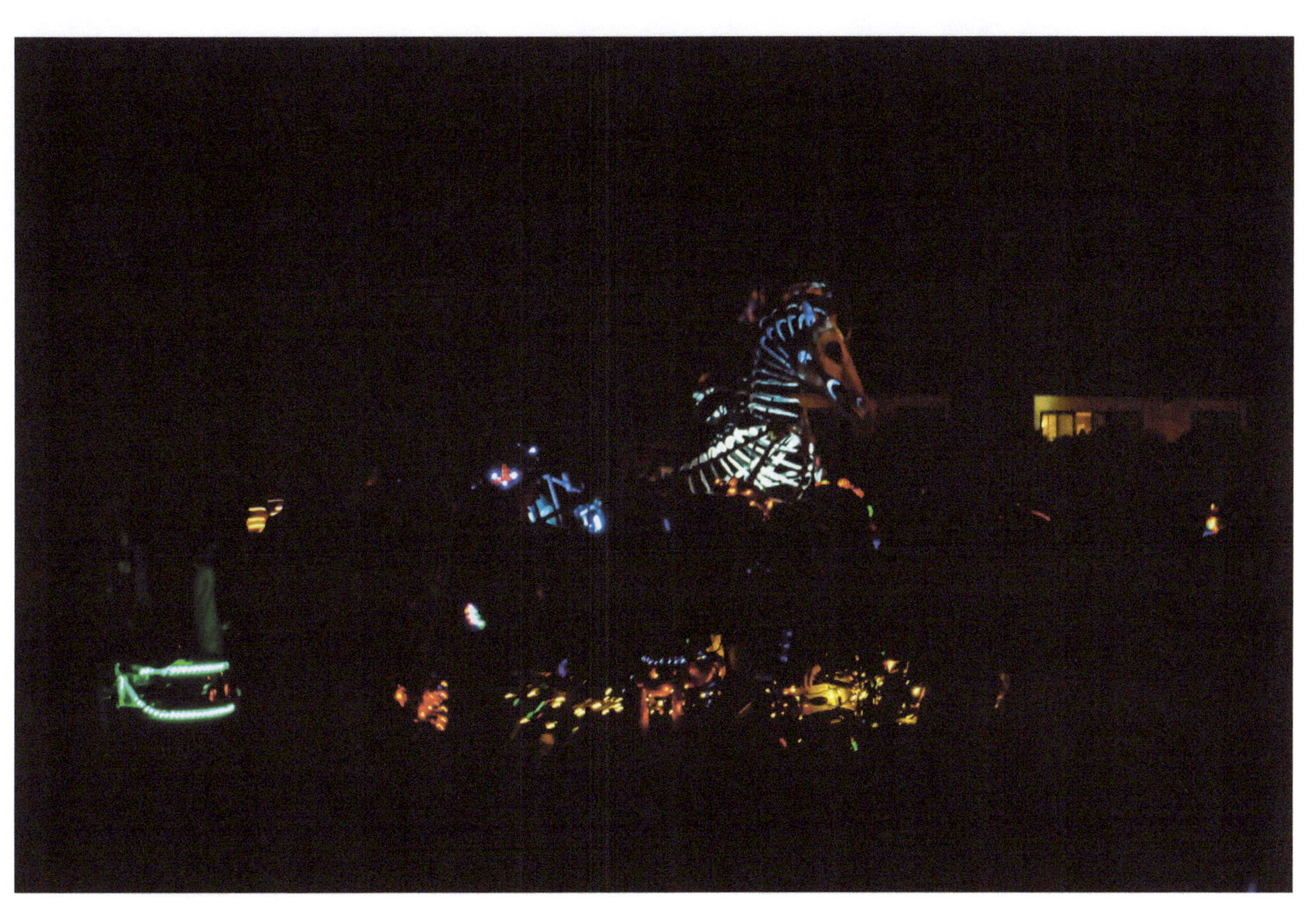

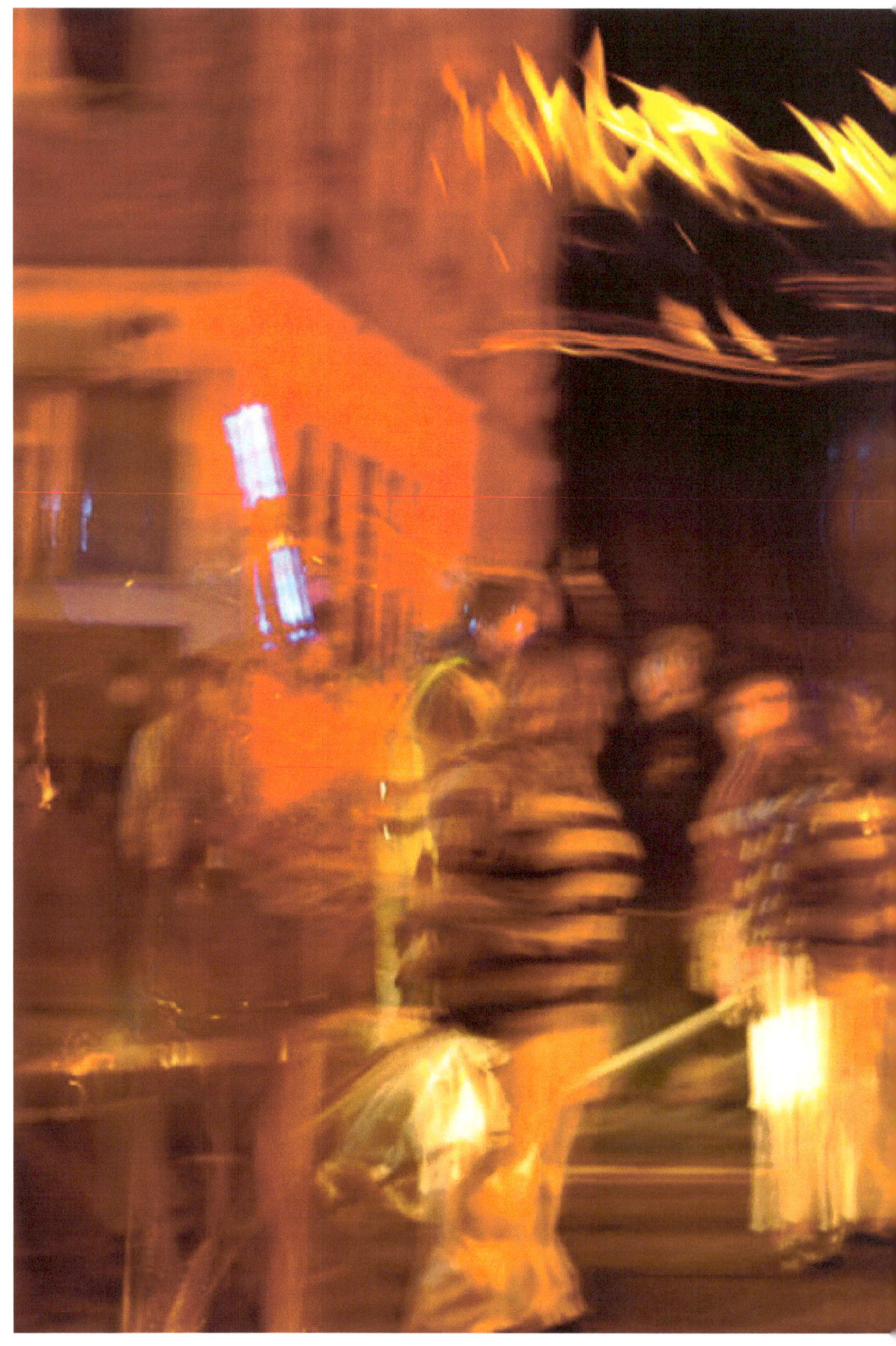

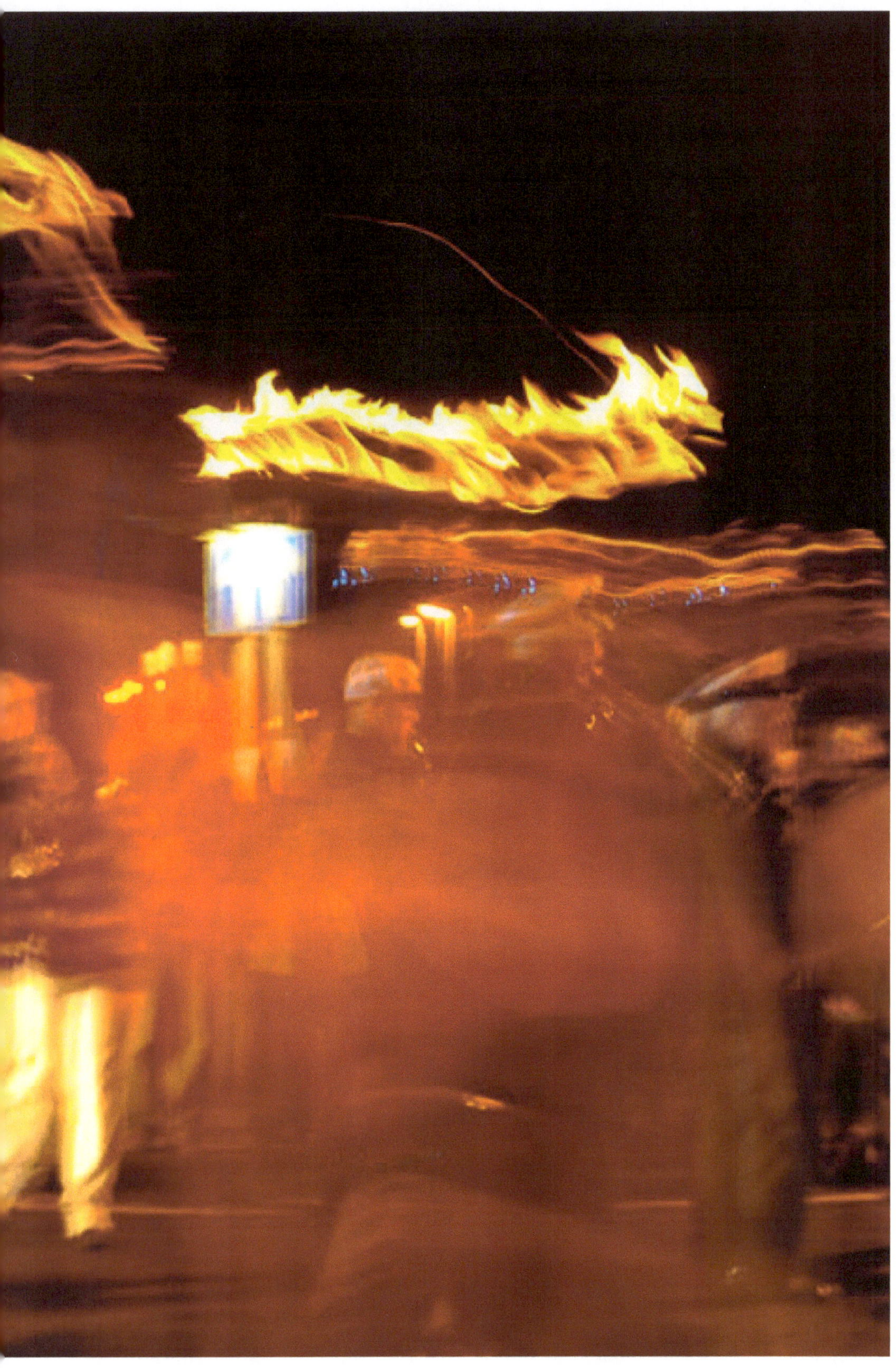

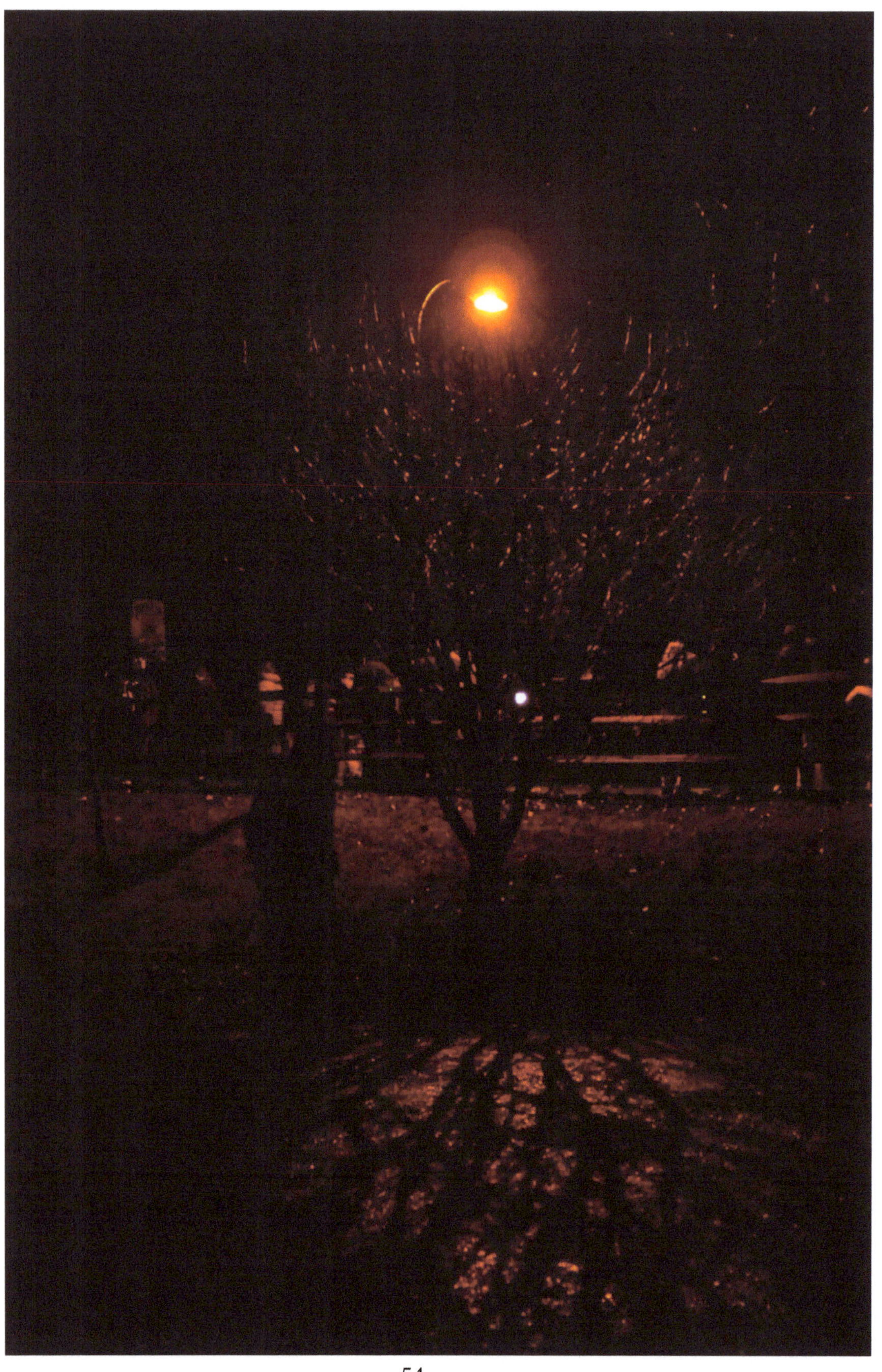

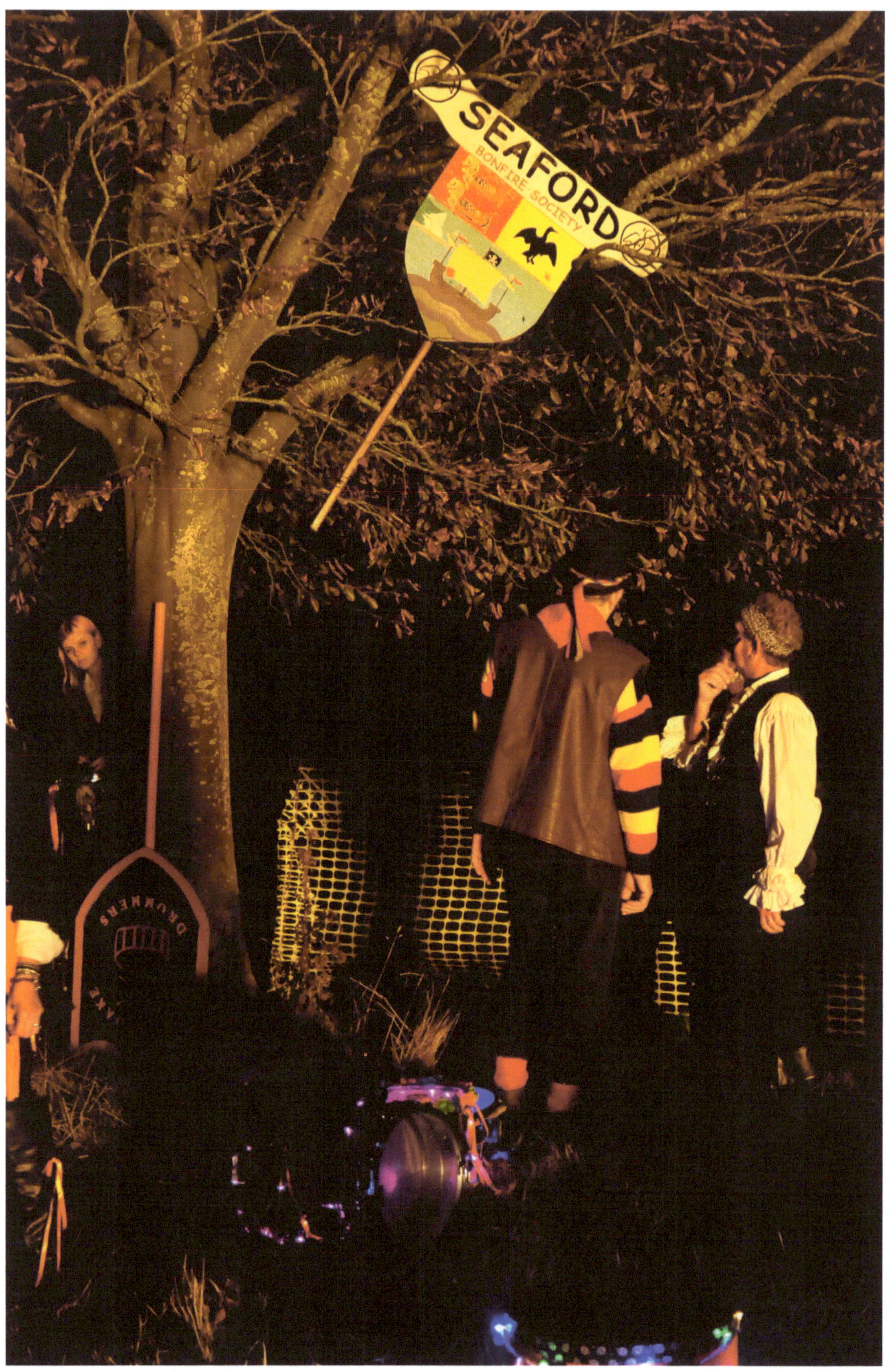

SEAFORD
BONFIRE SOCIETY
DRUMMERS

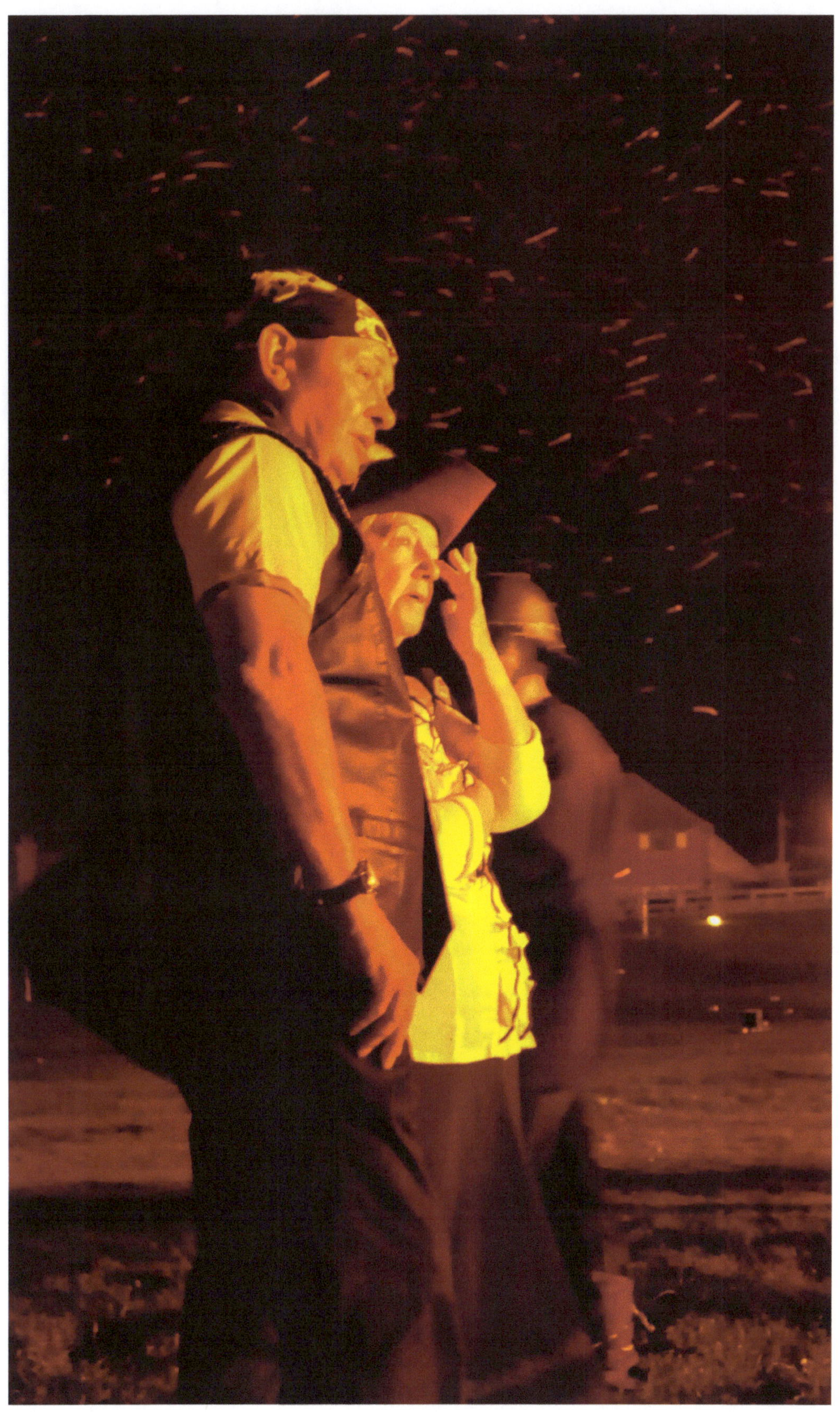

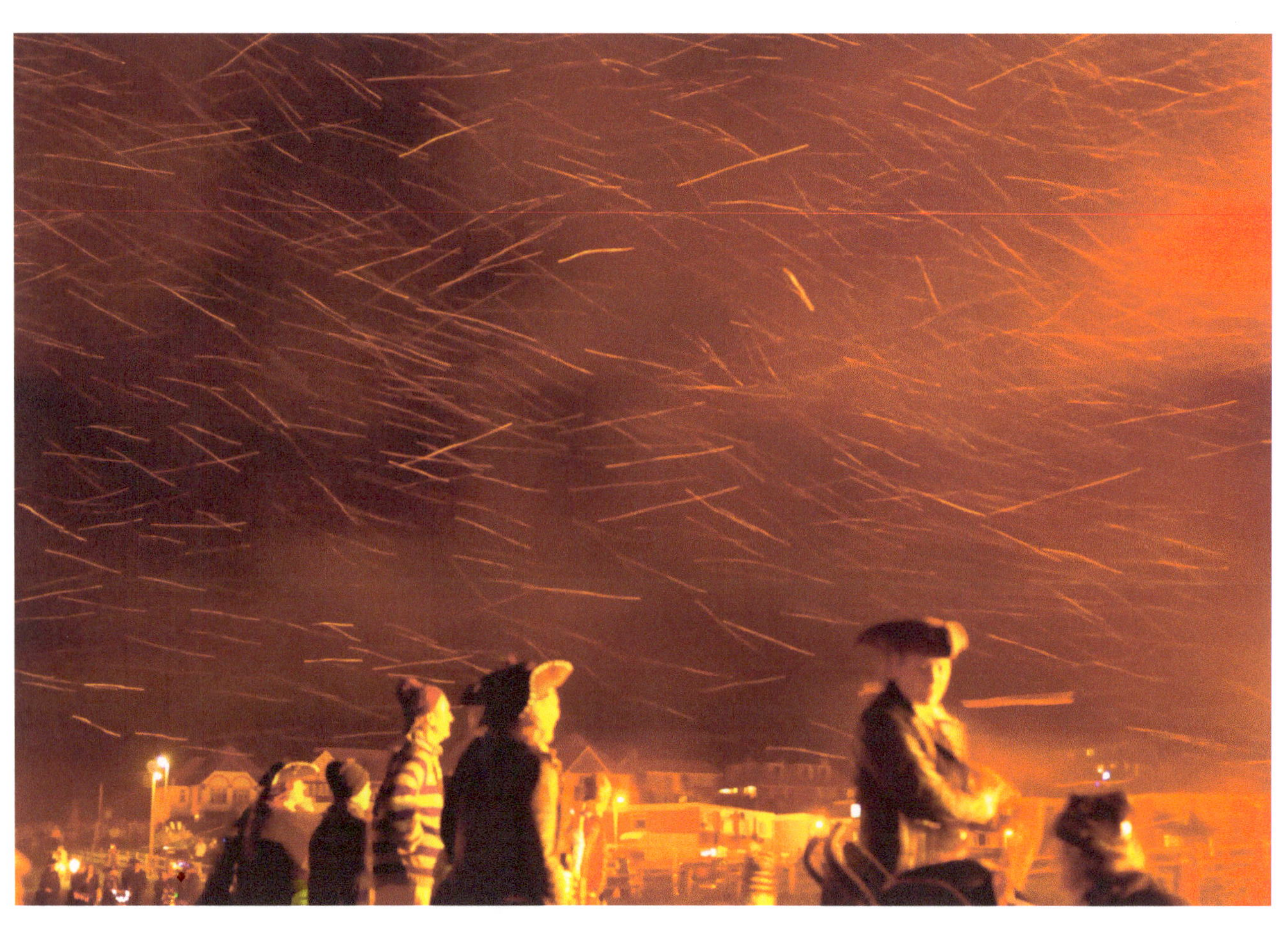

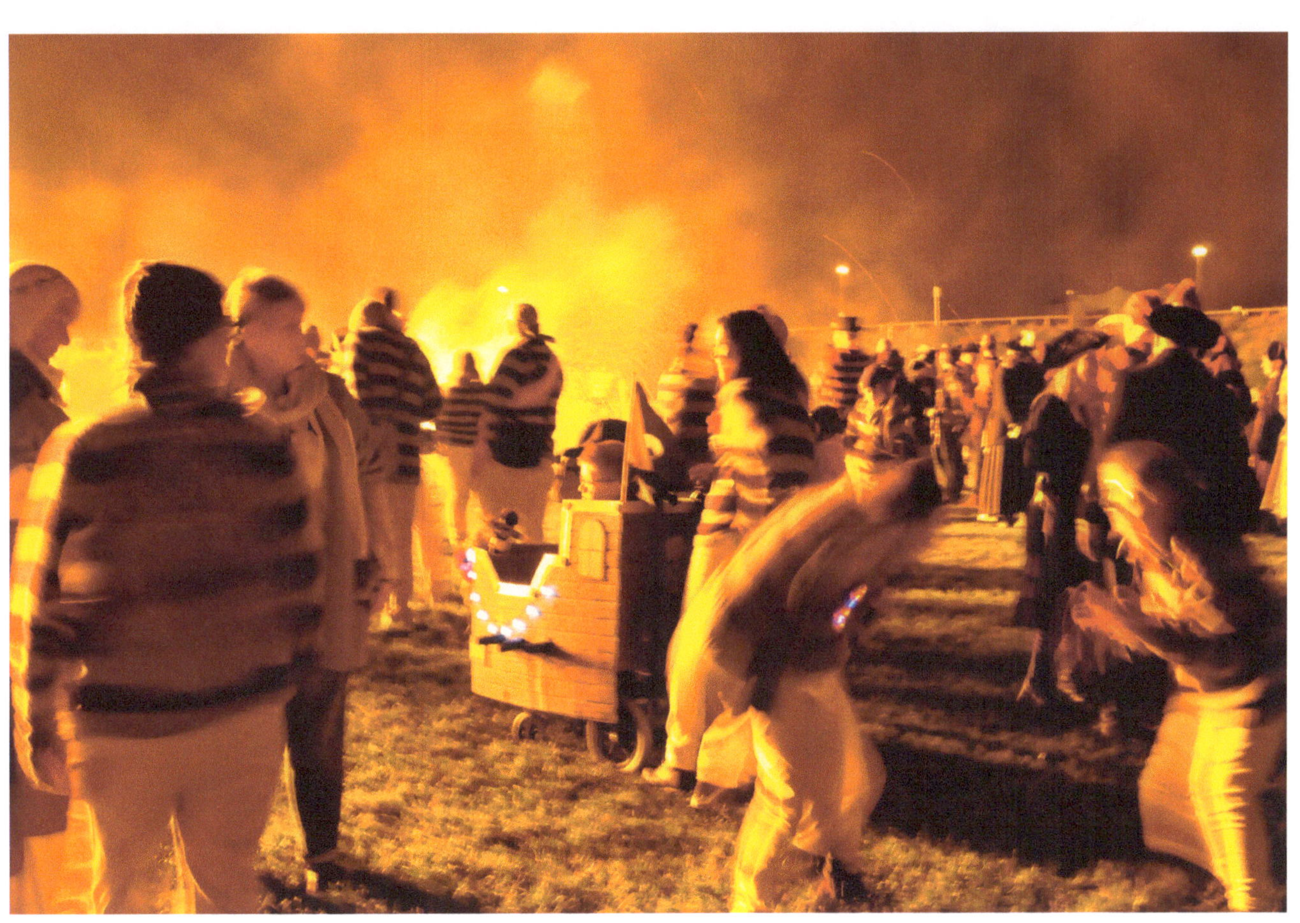

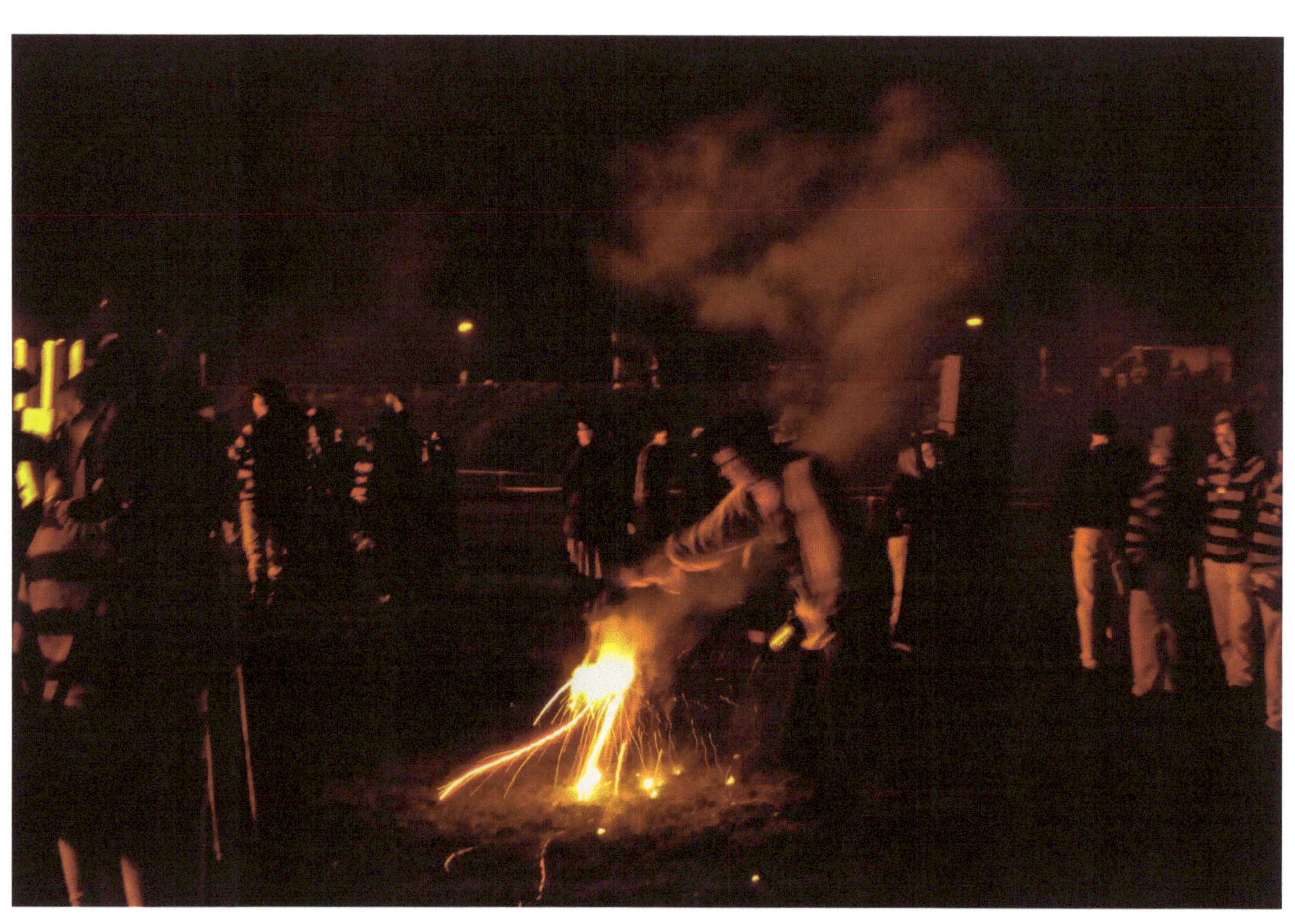

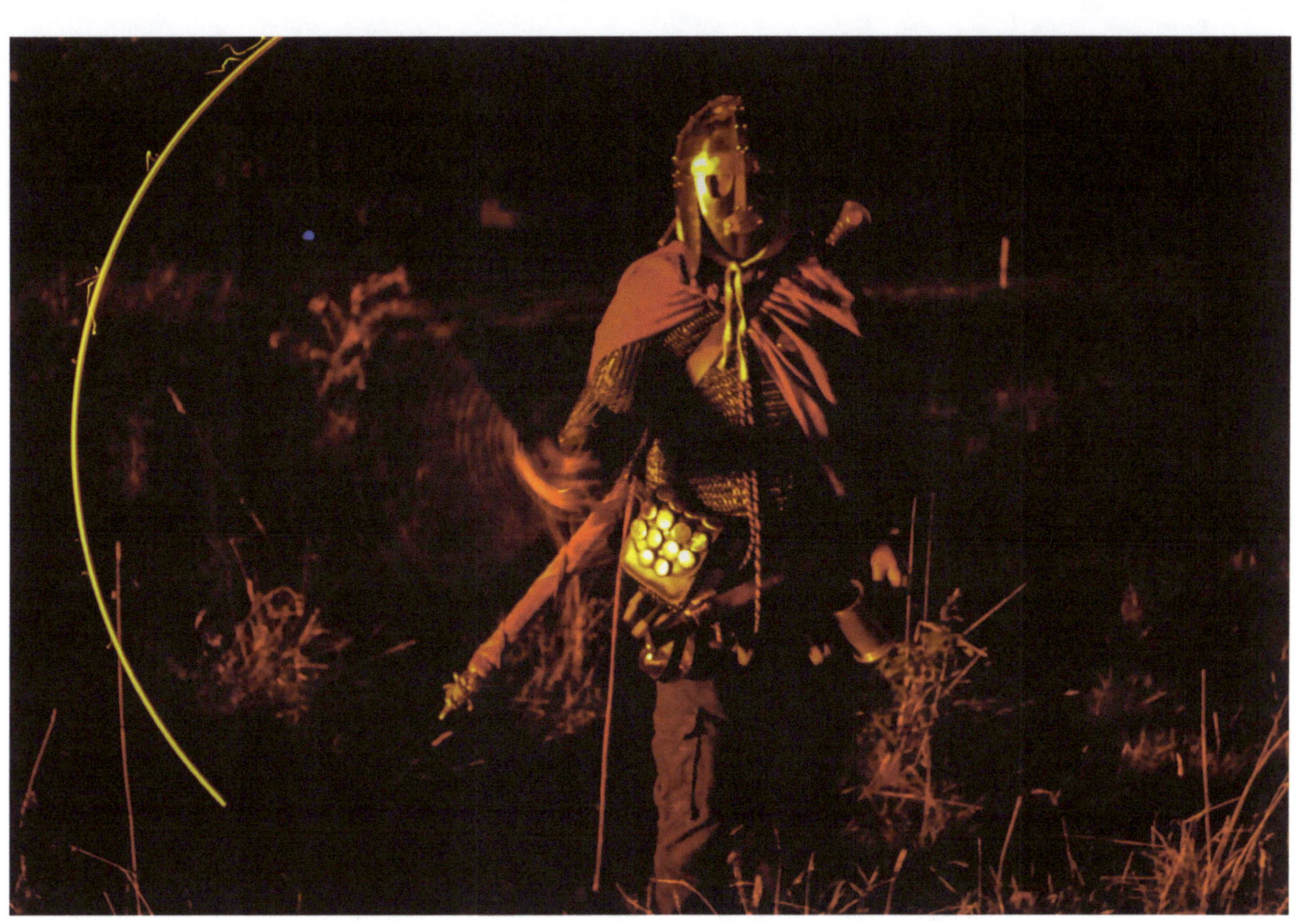

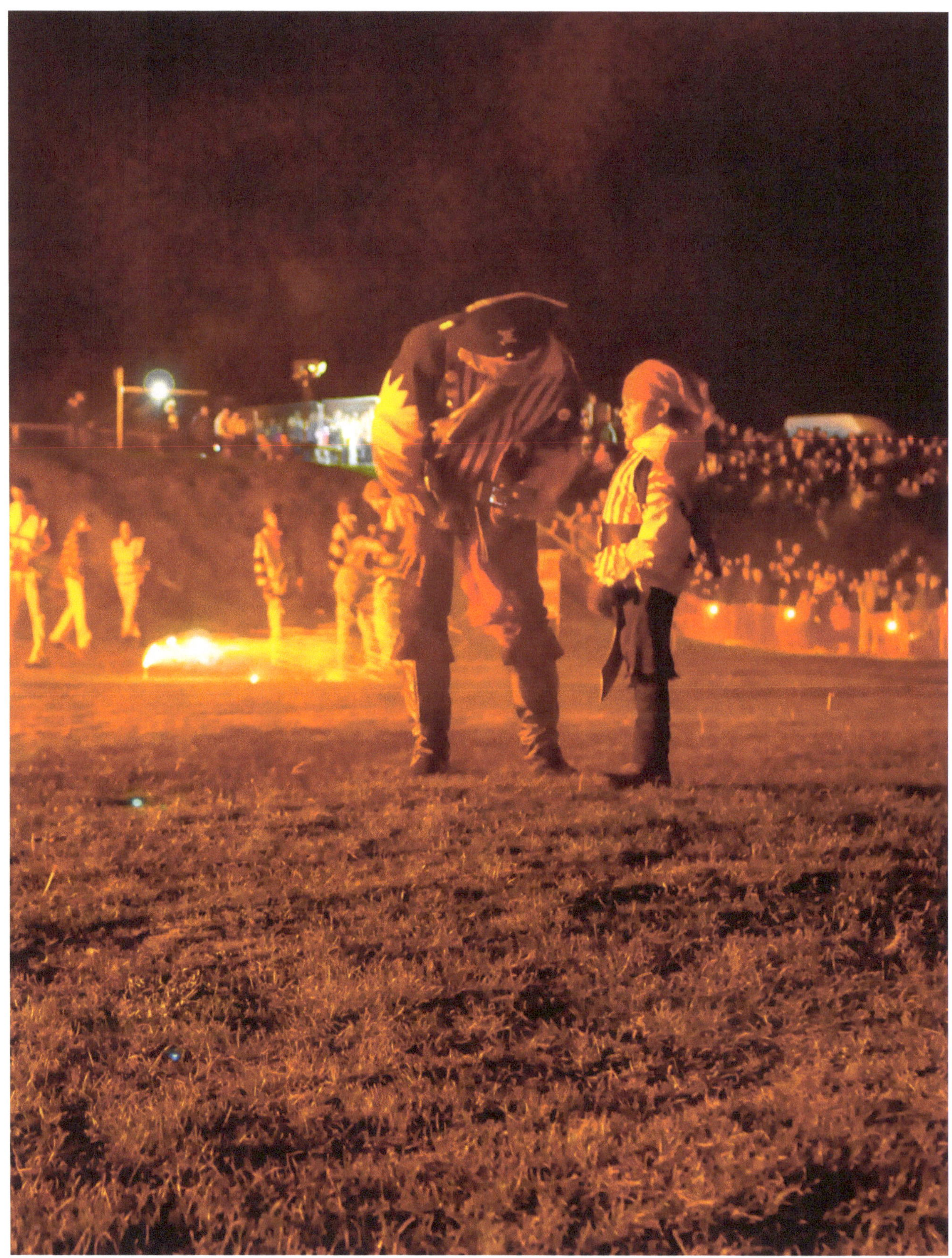

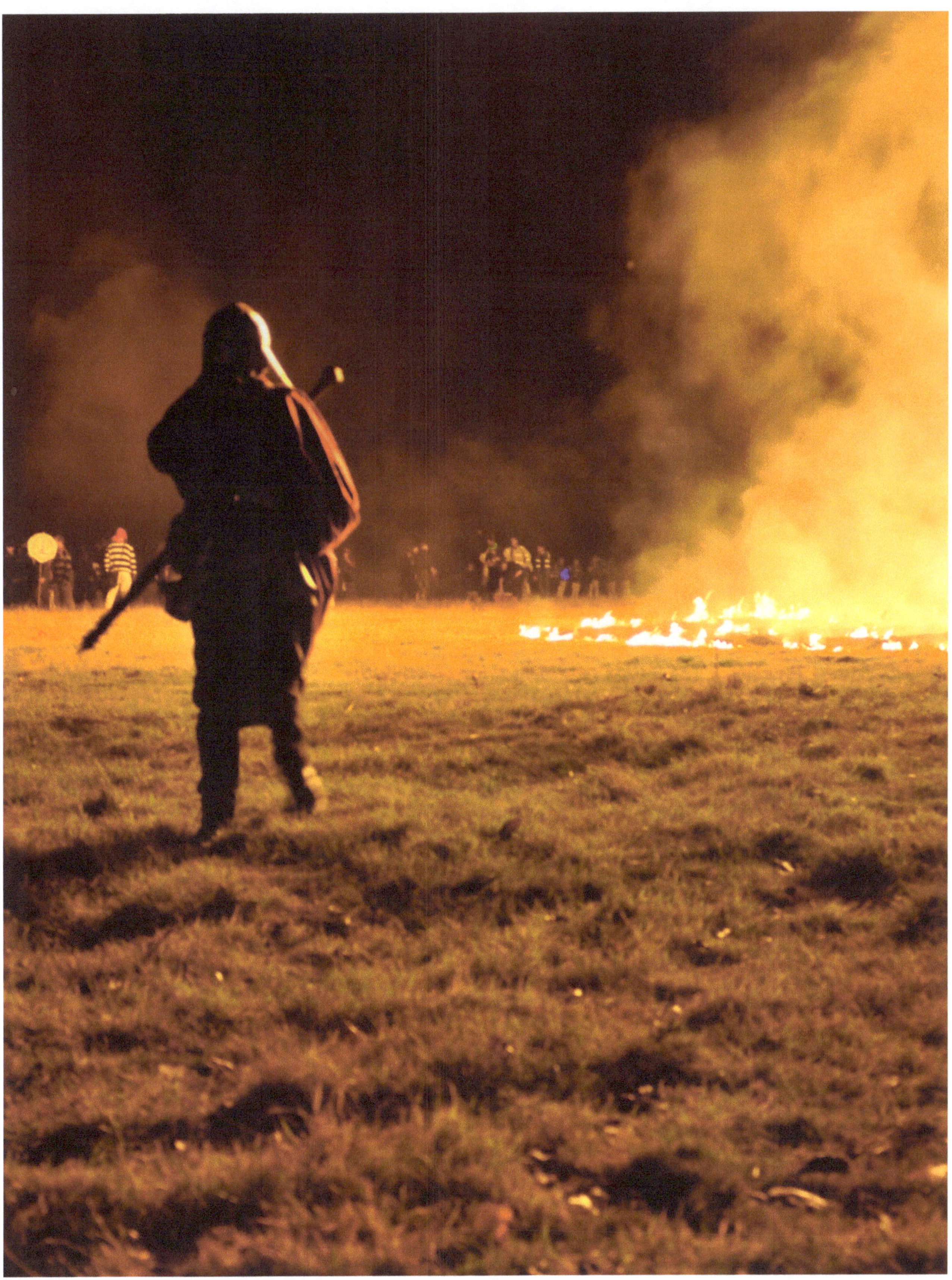

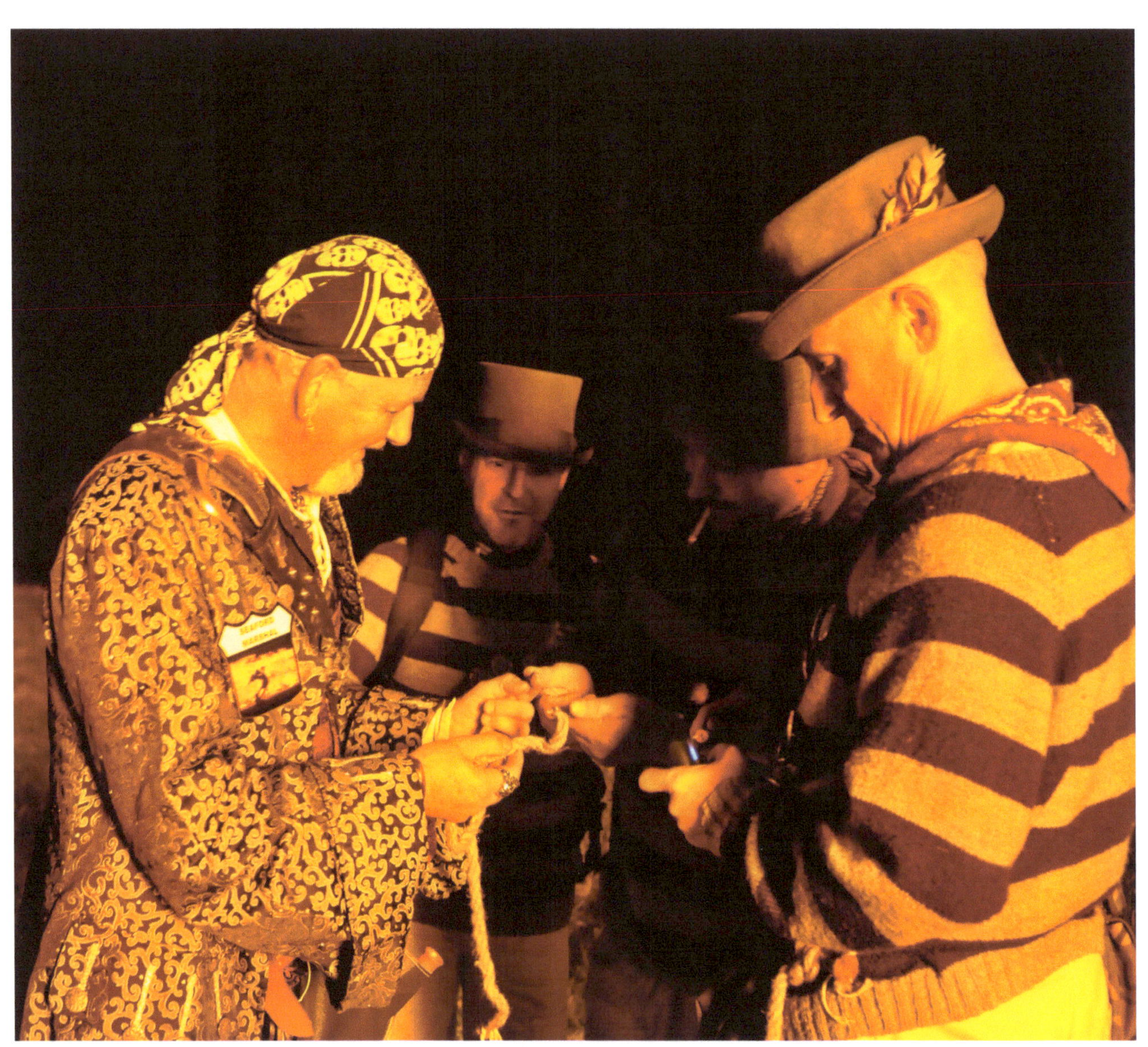

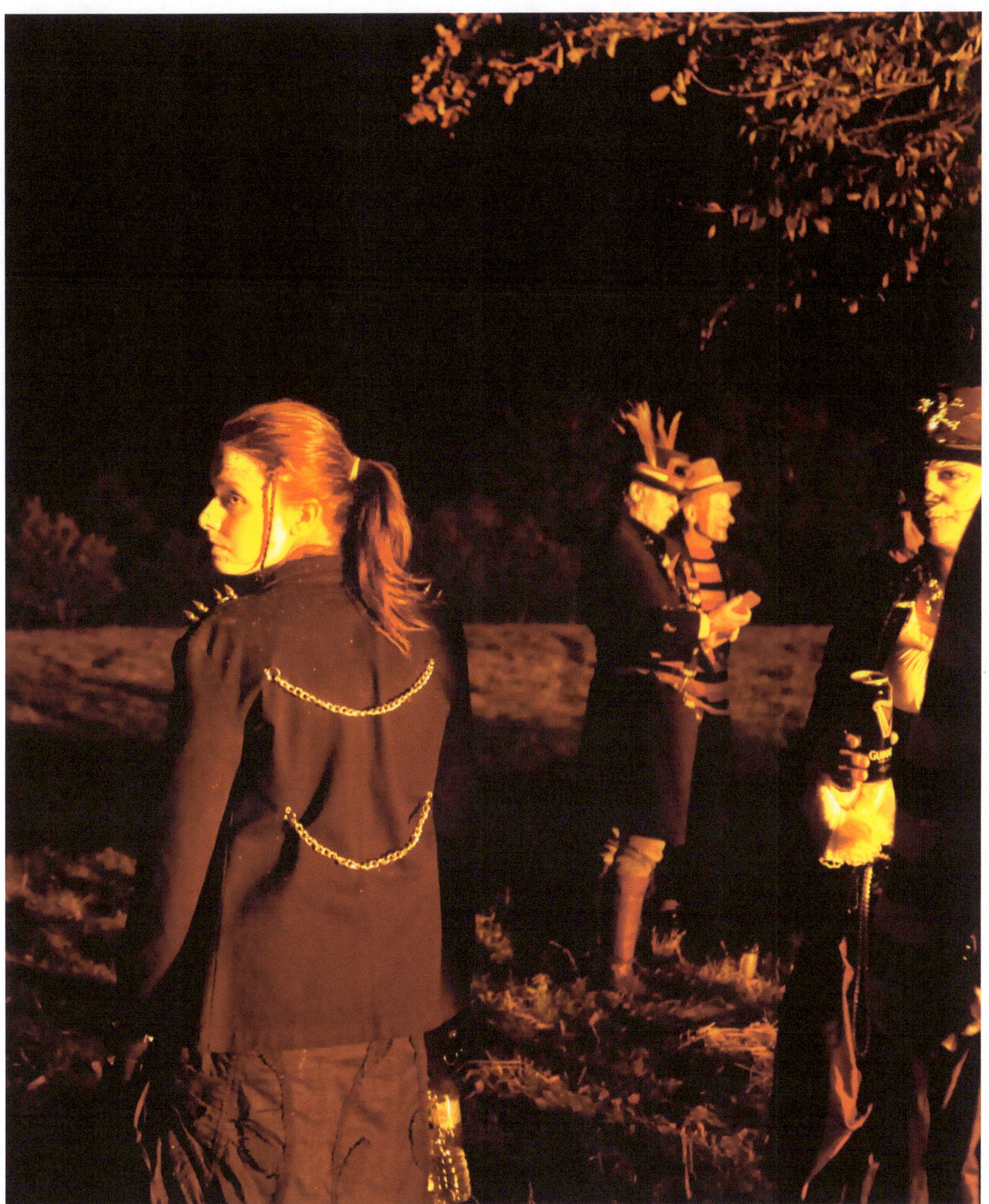

Bonfire

"The bigger you build the bonfire, the more darkness is revealed."

Terence McKenna

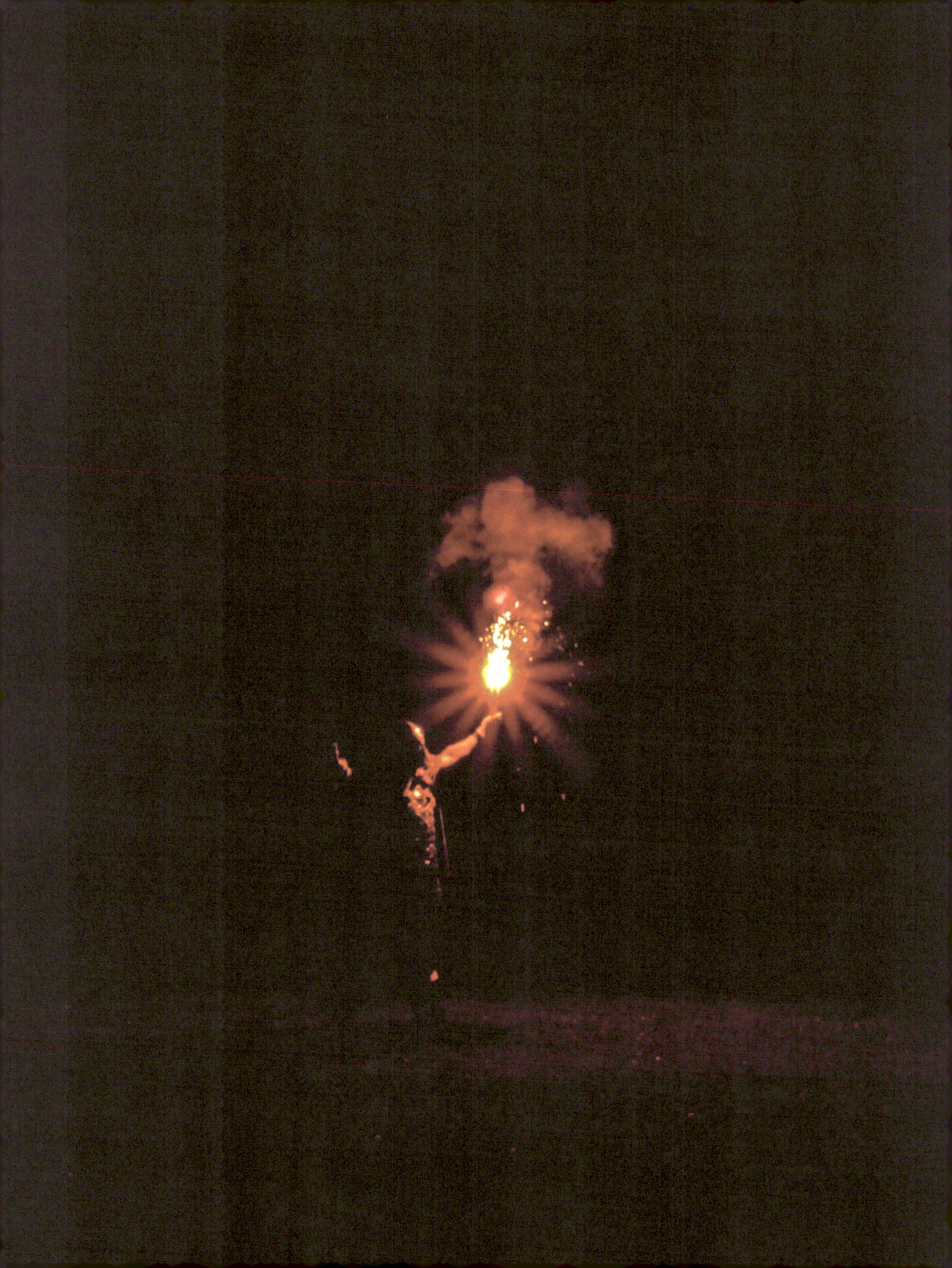

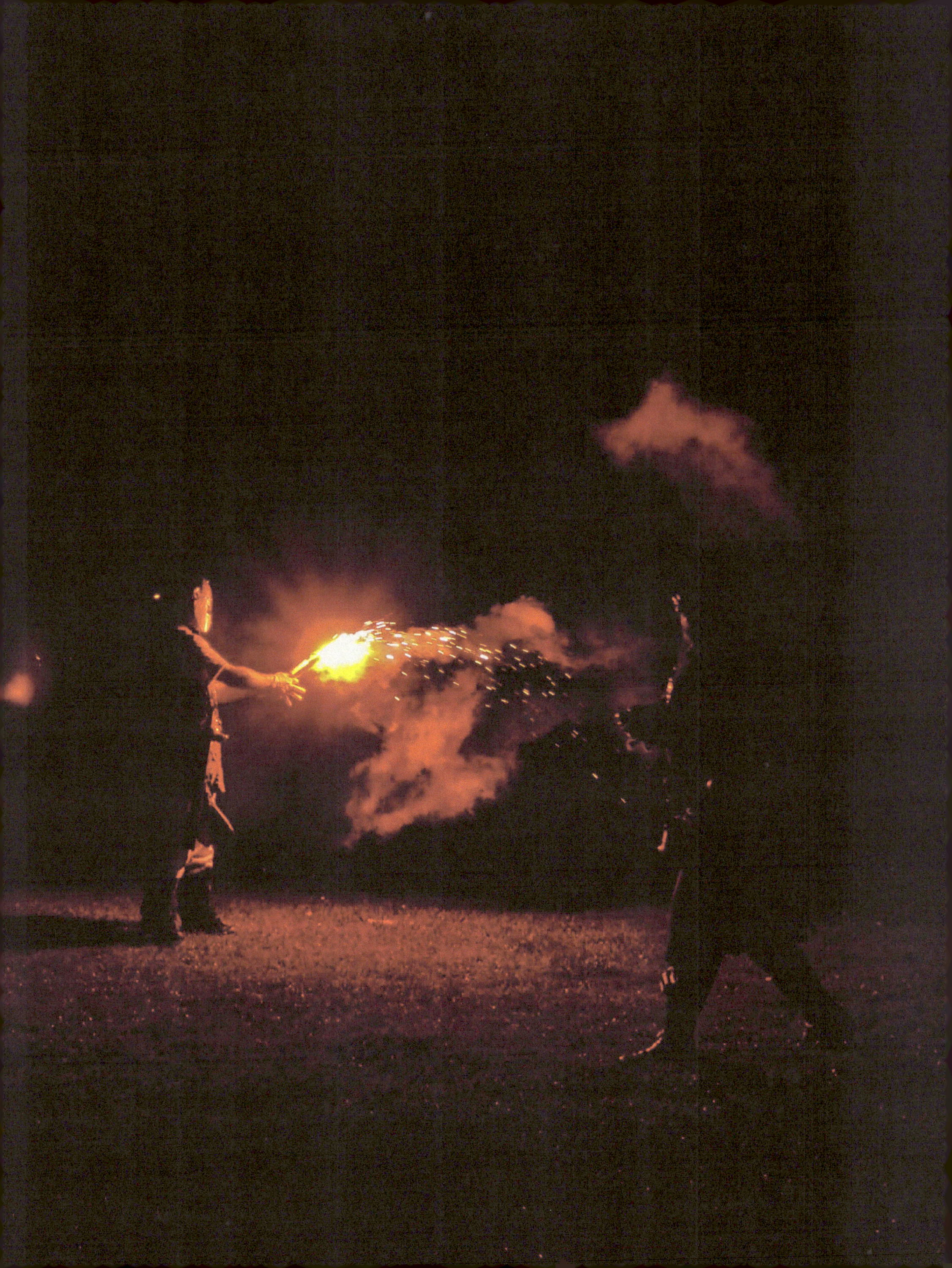

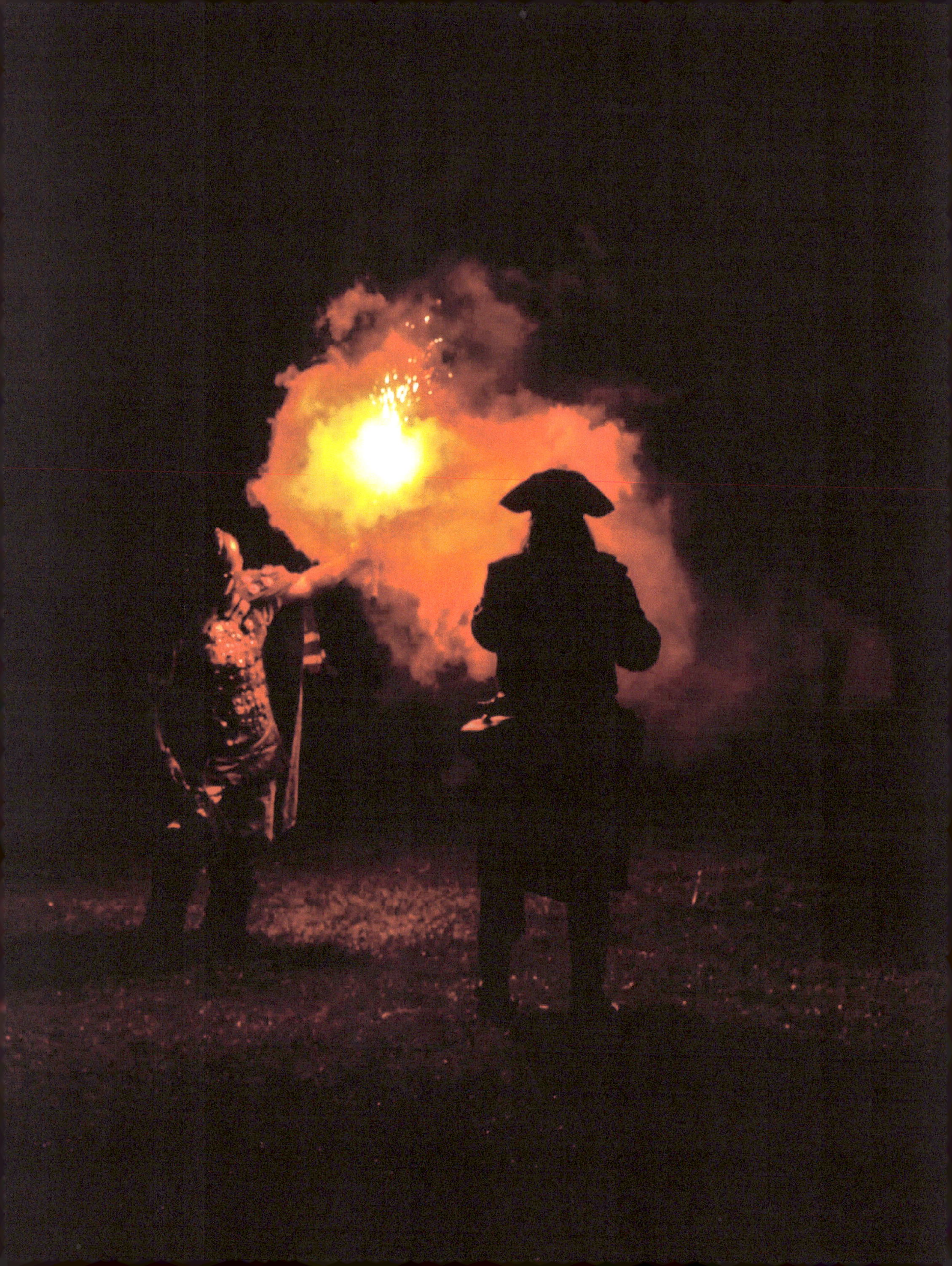

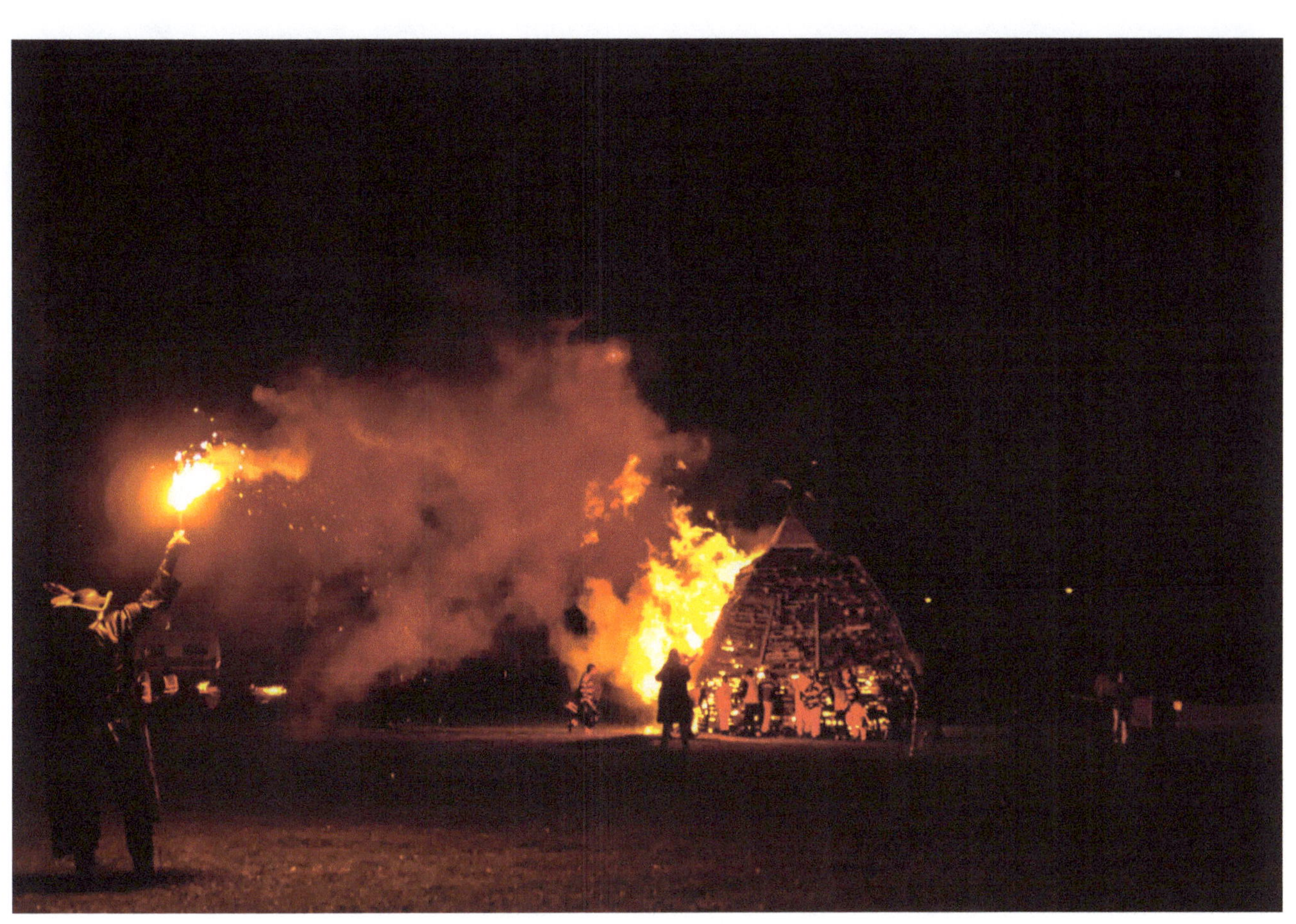

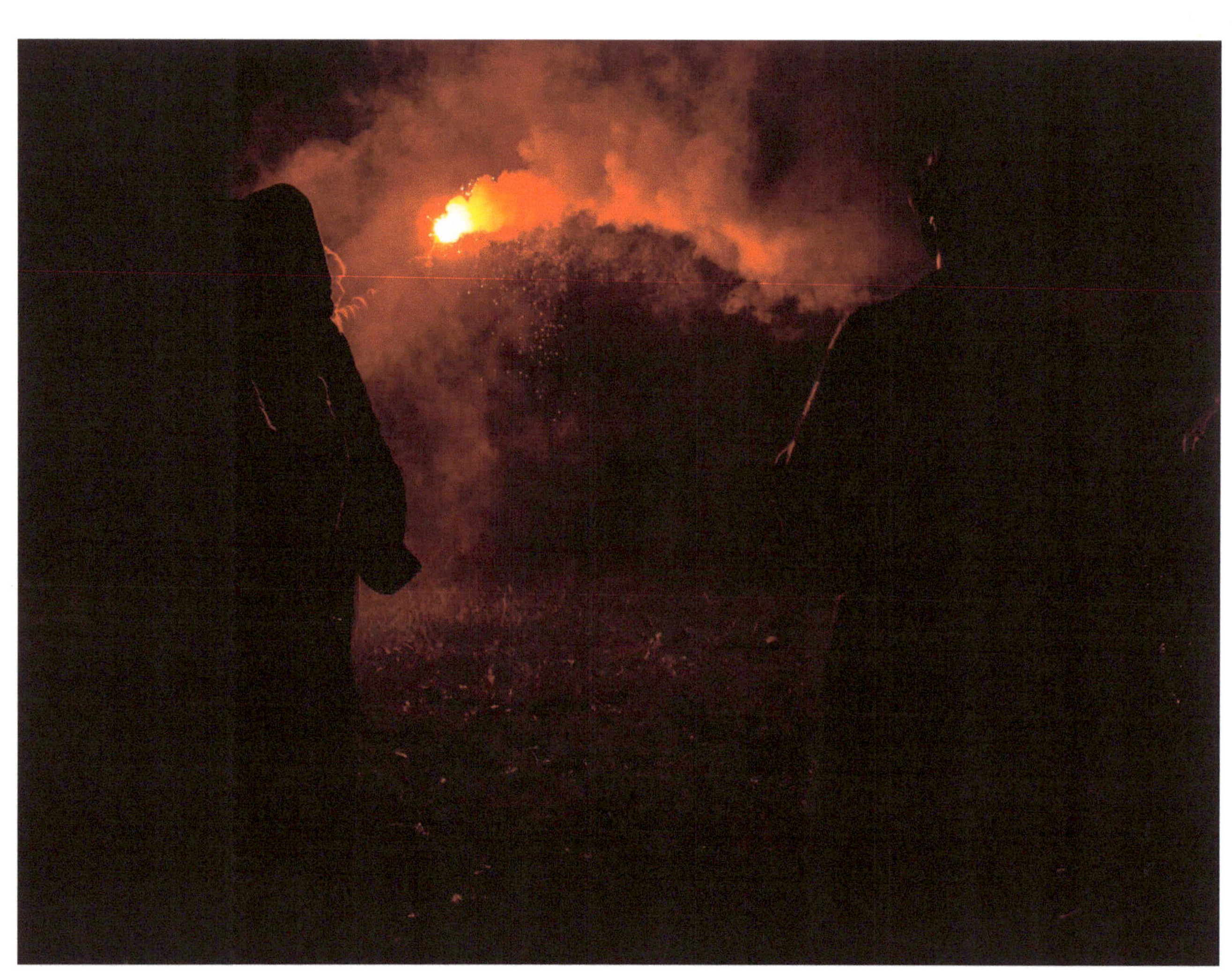

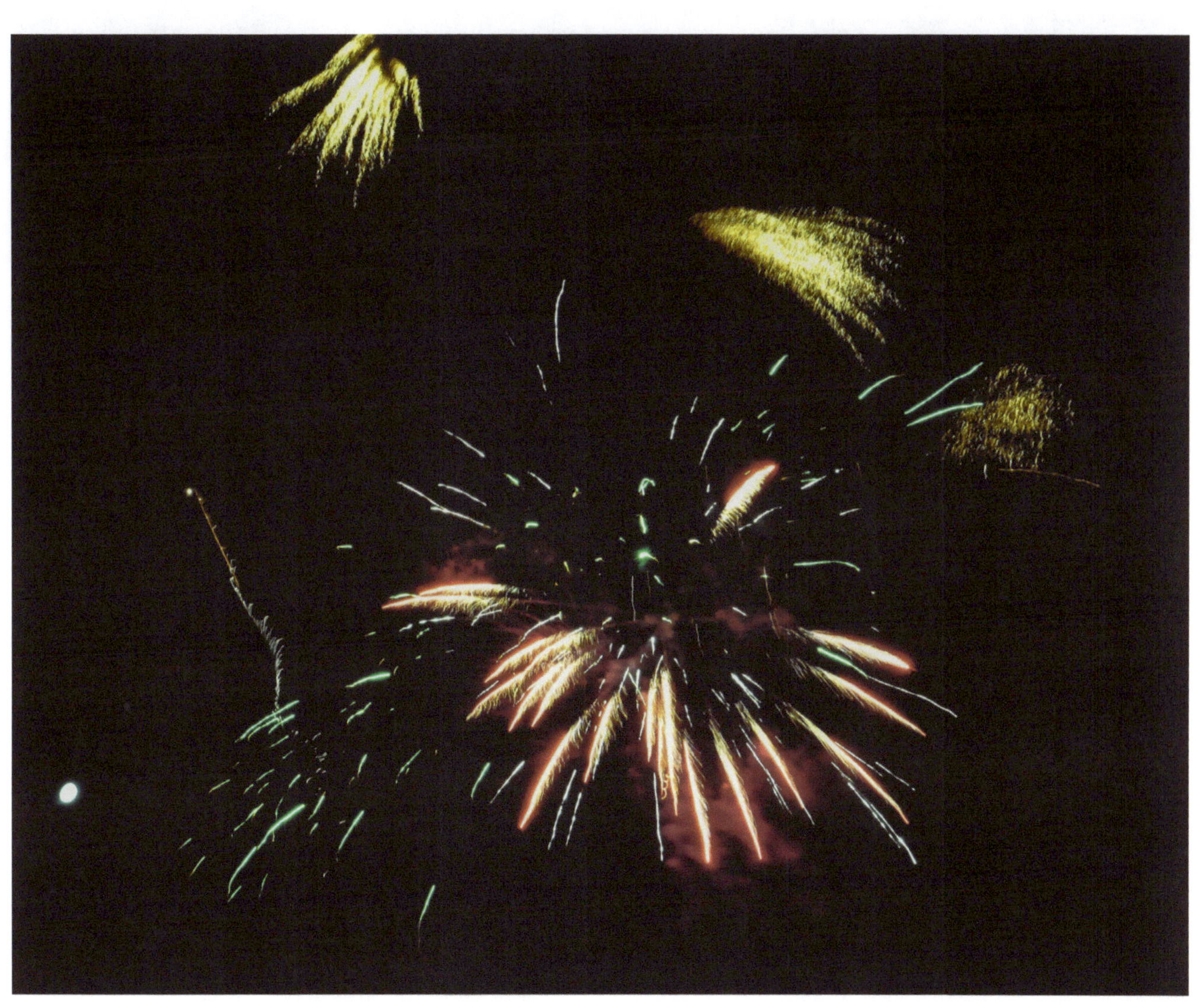

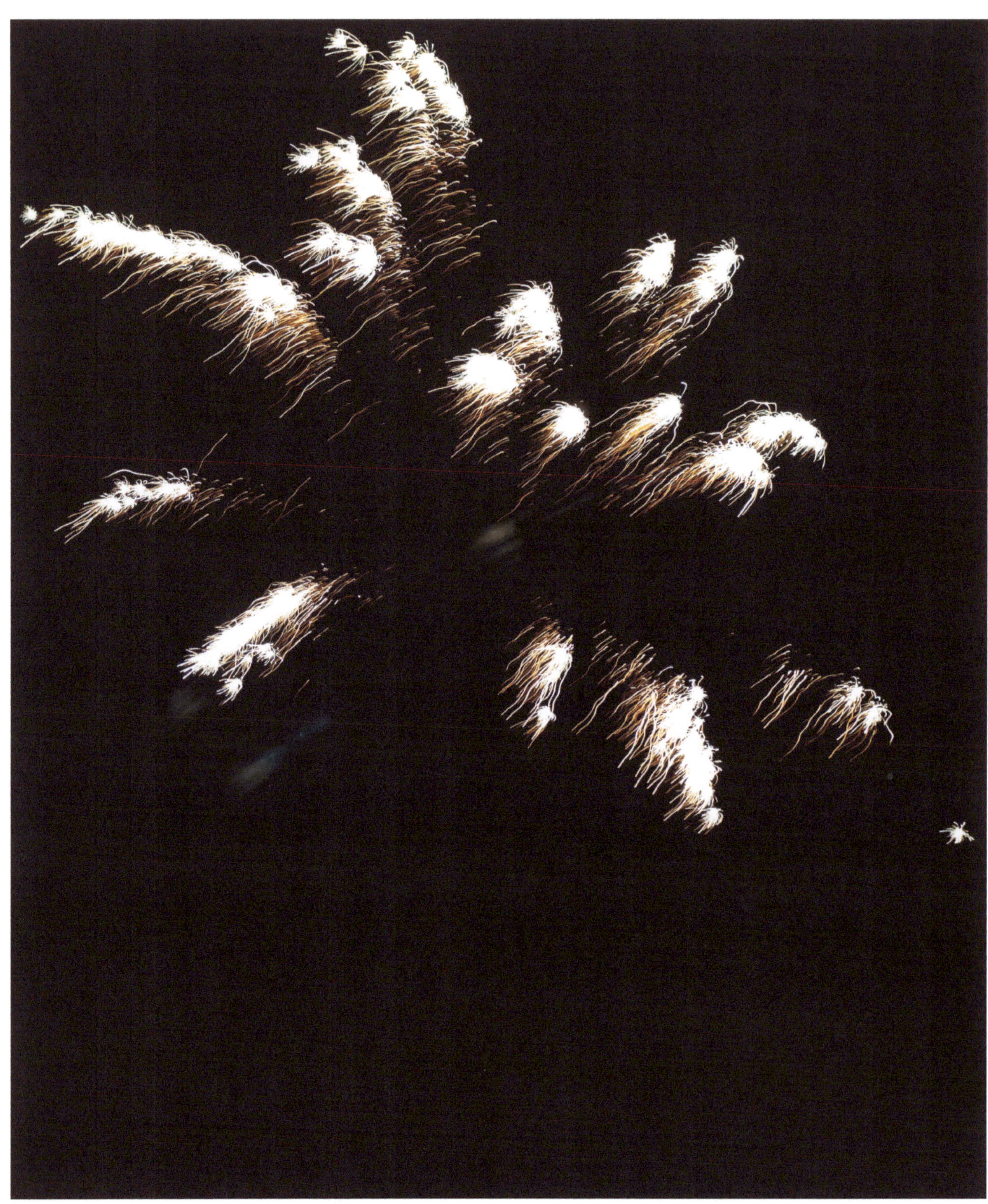

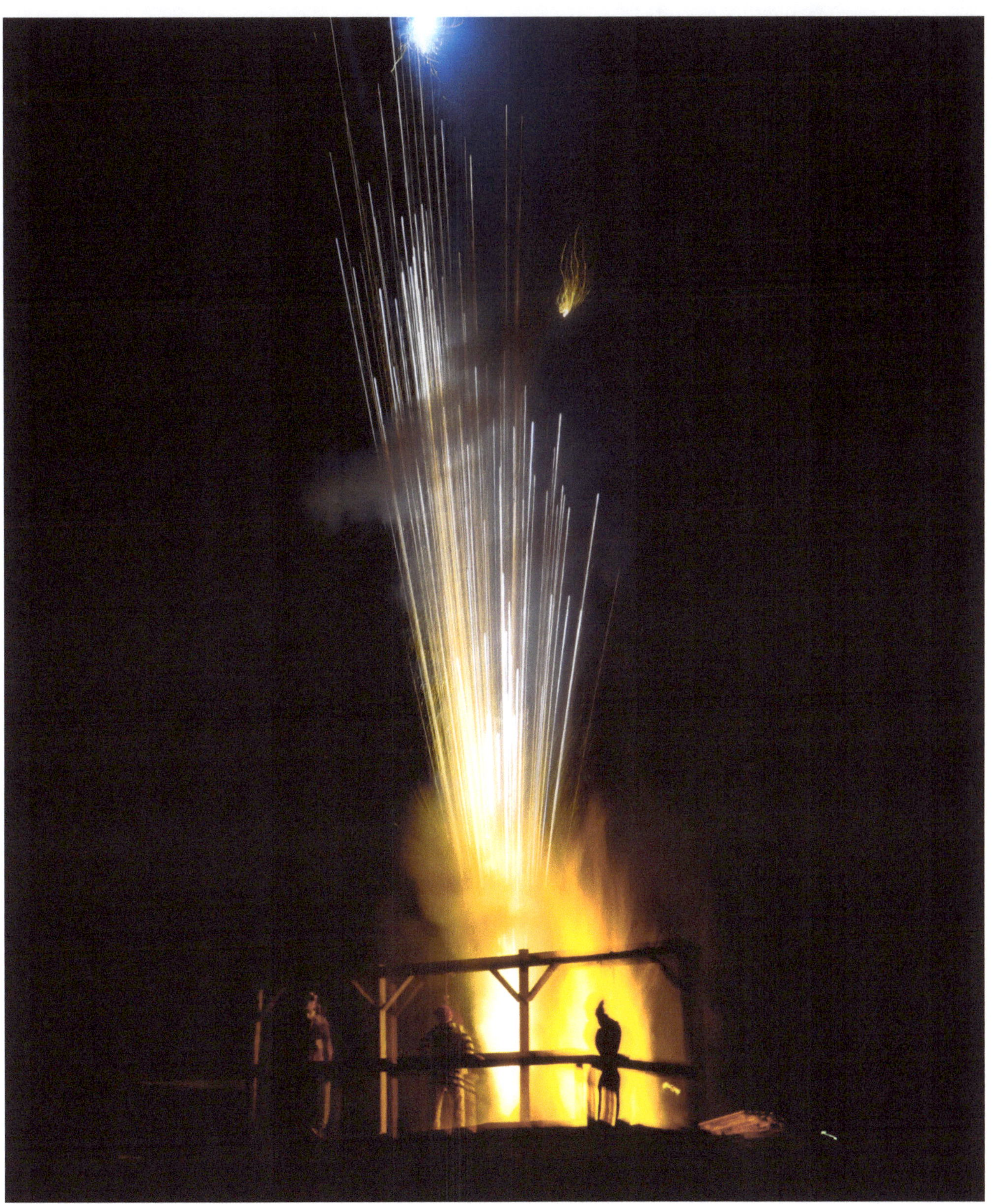

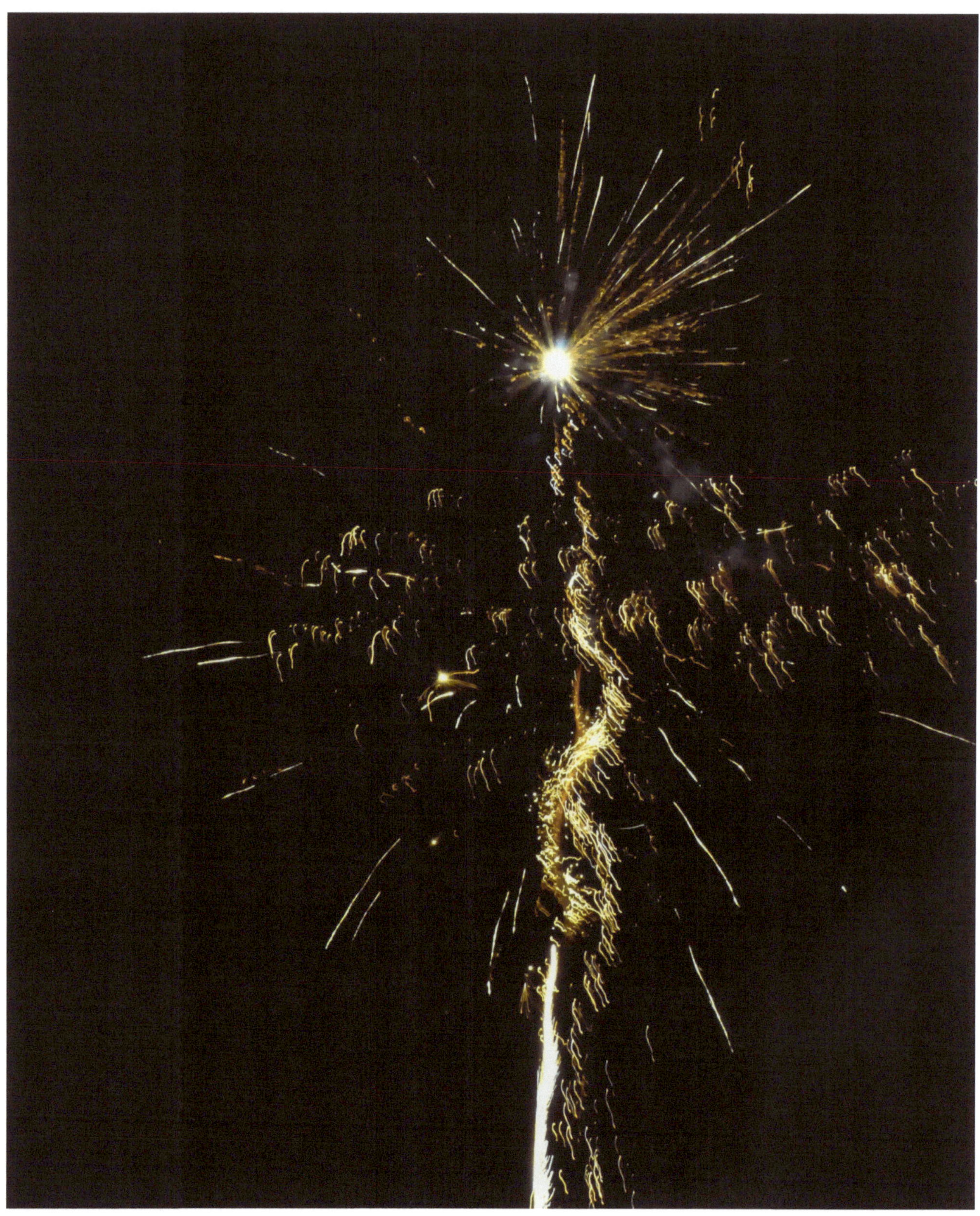

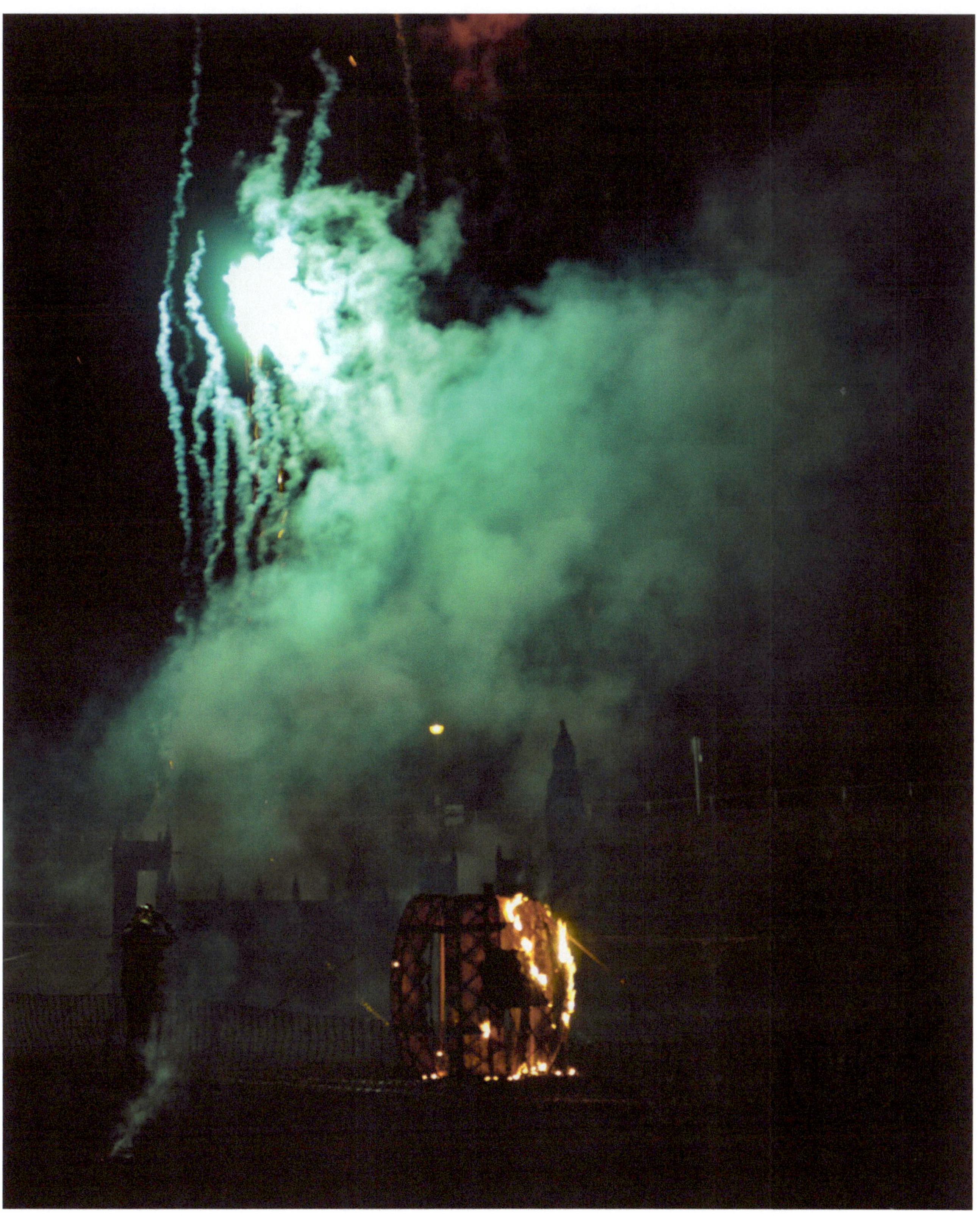

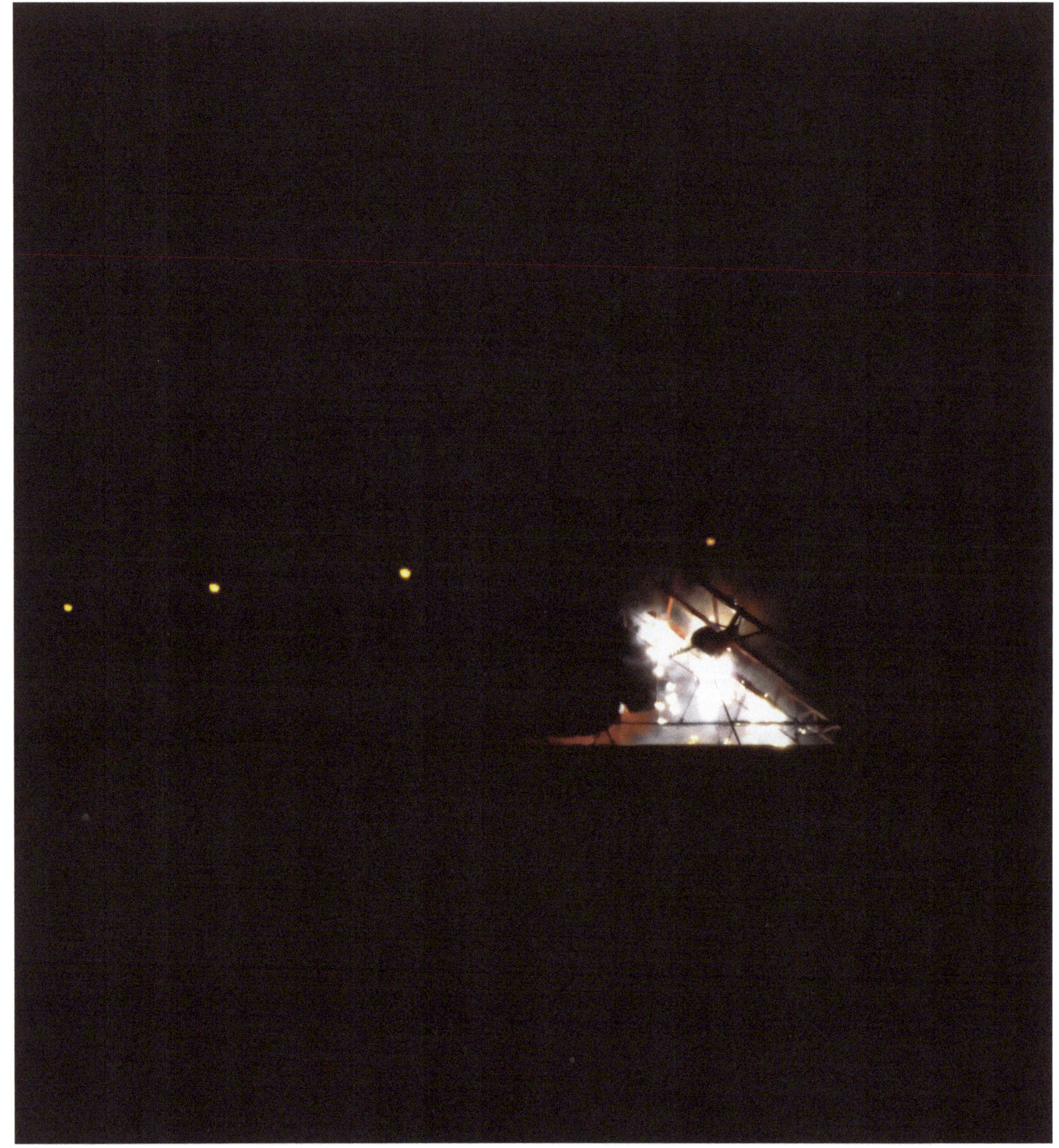

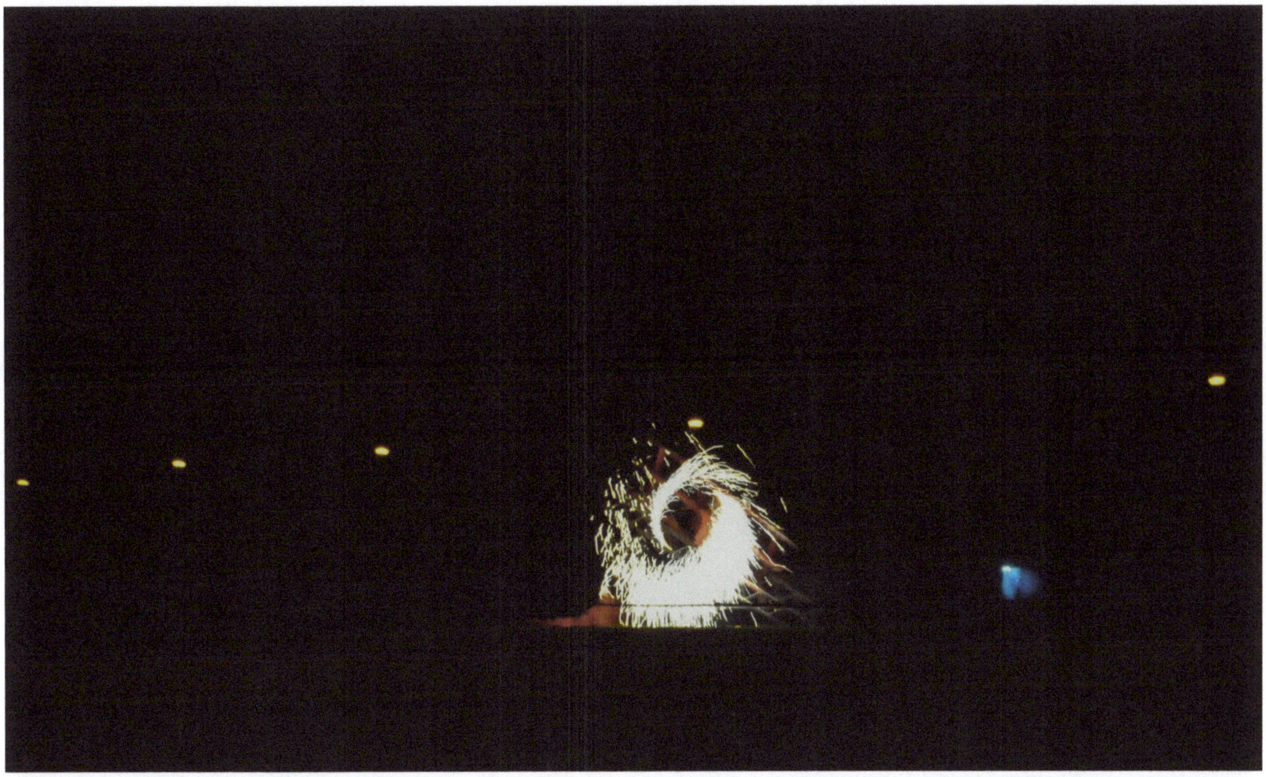

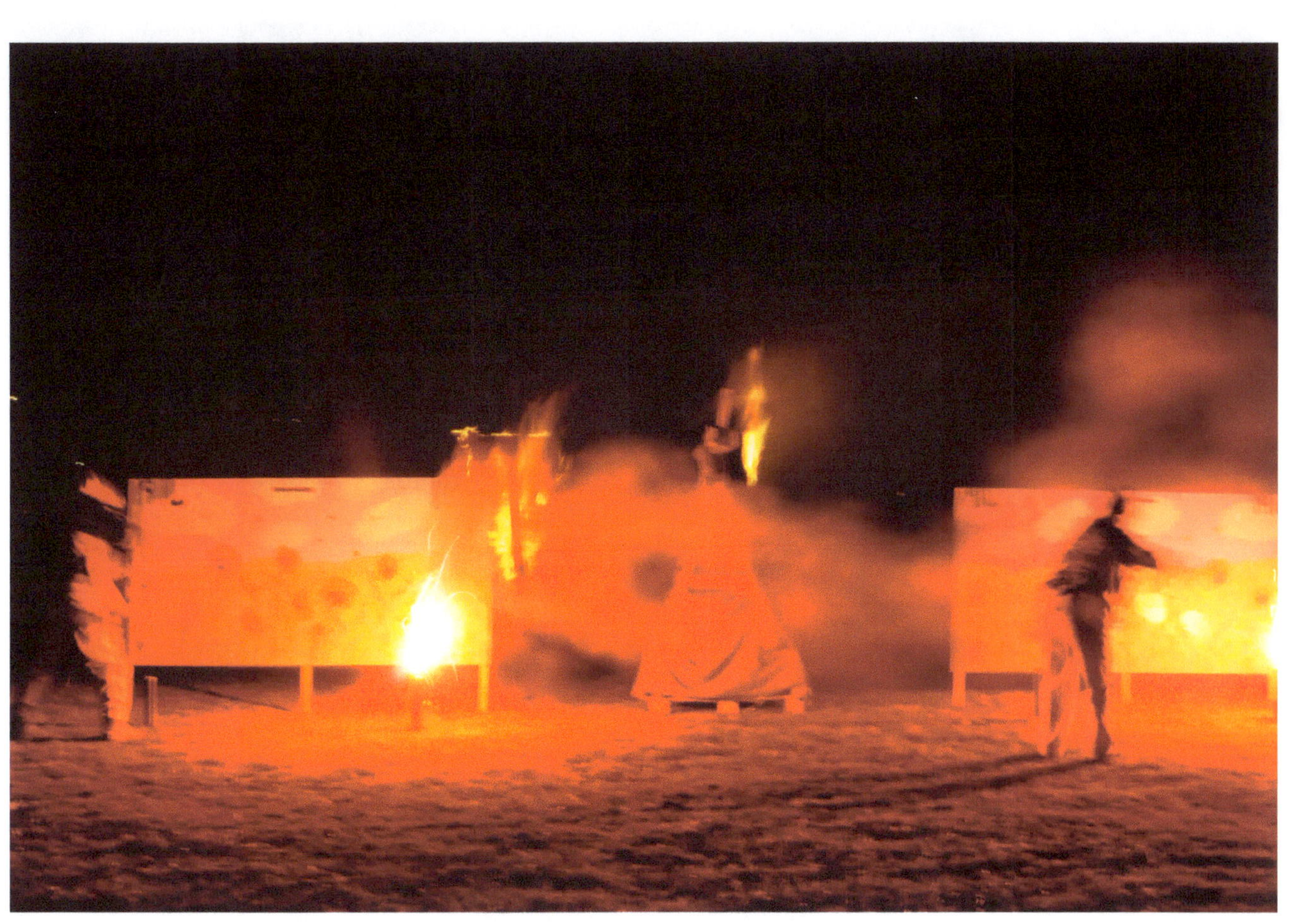

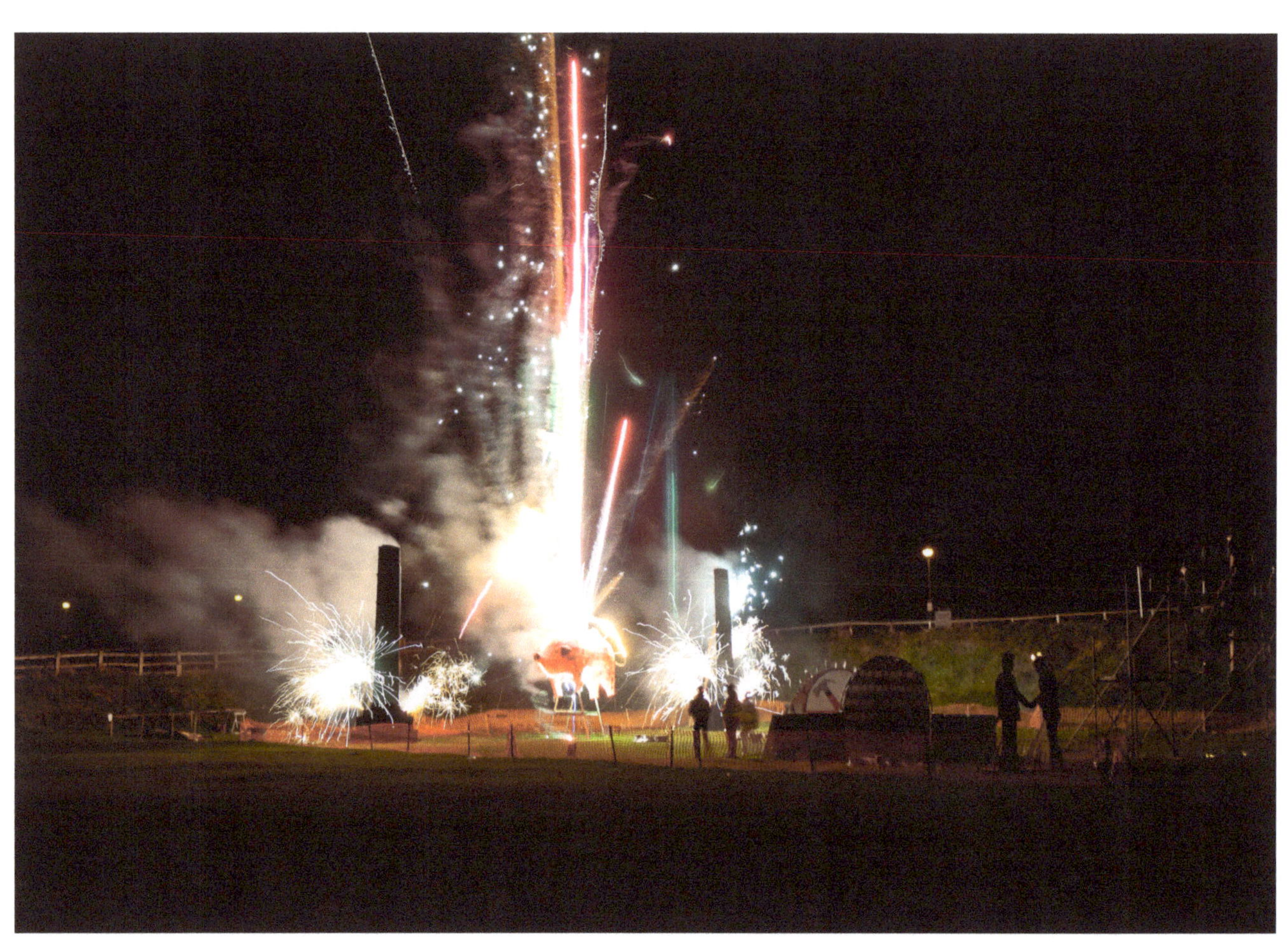

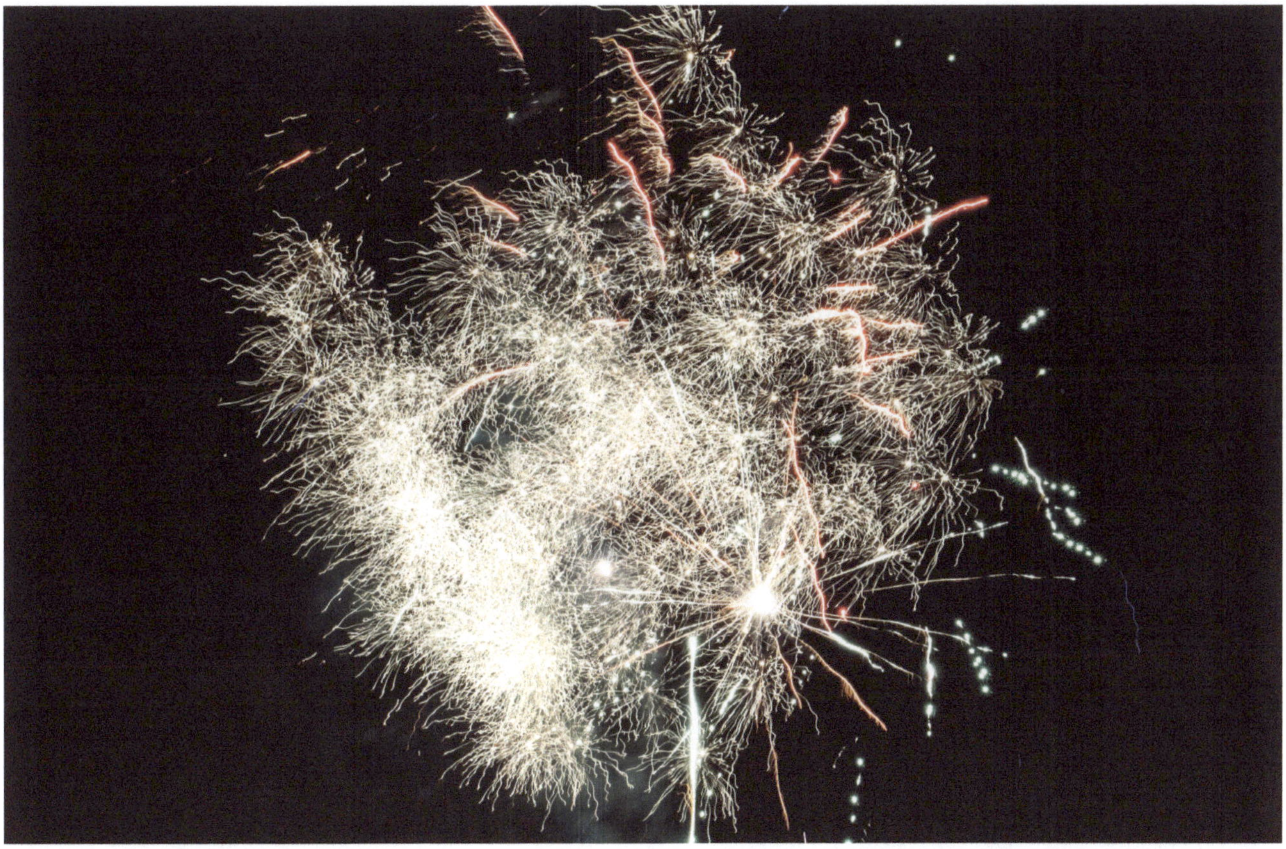

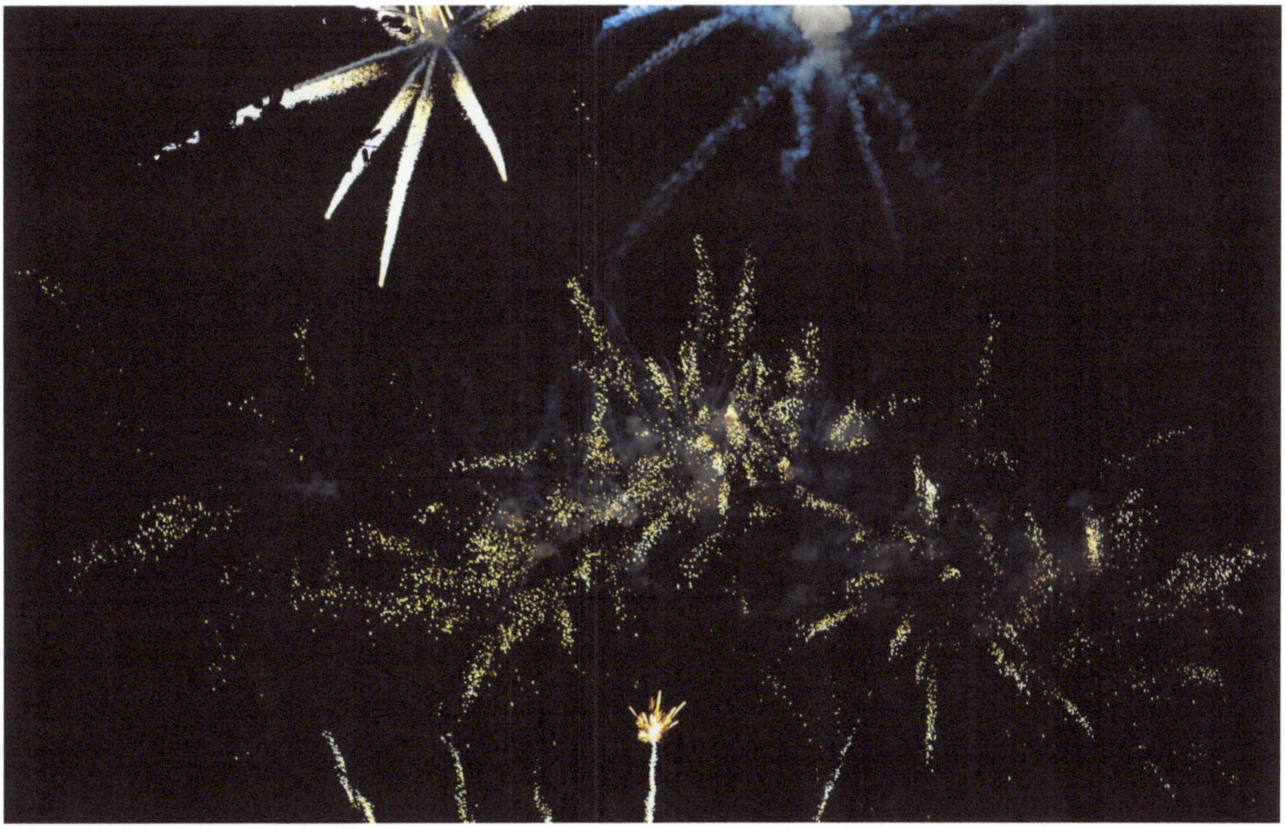

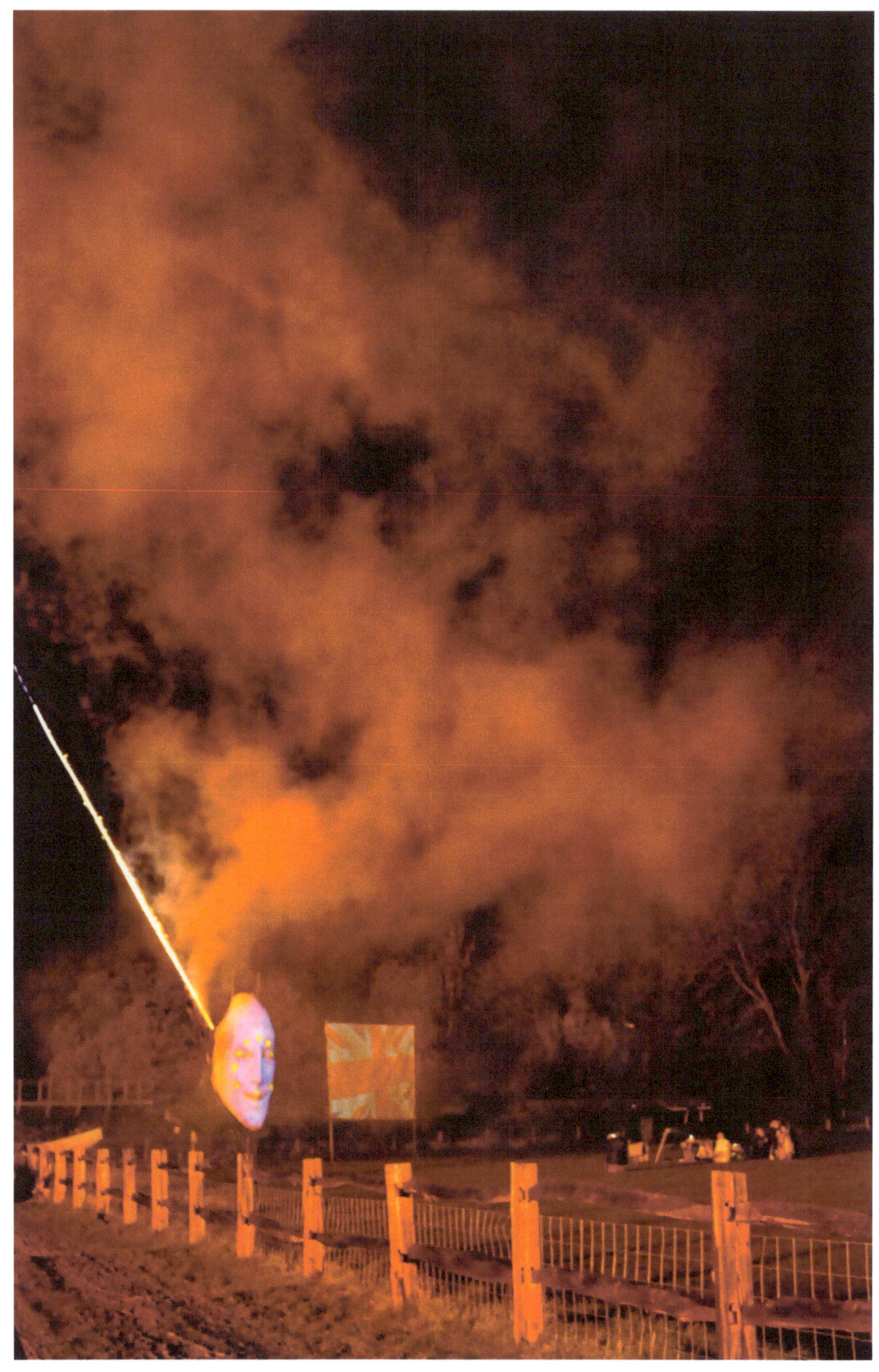

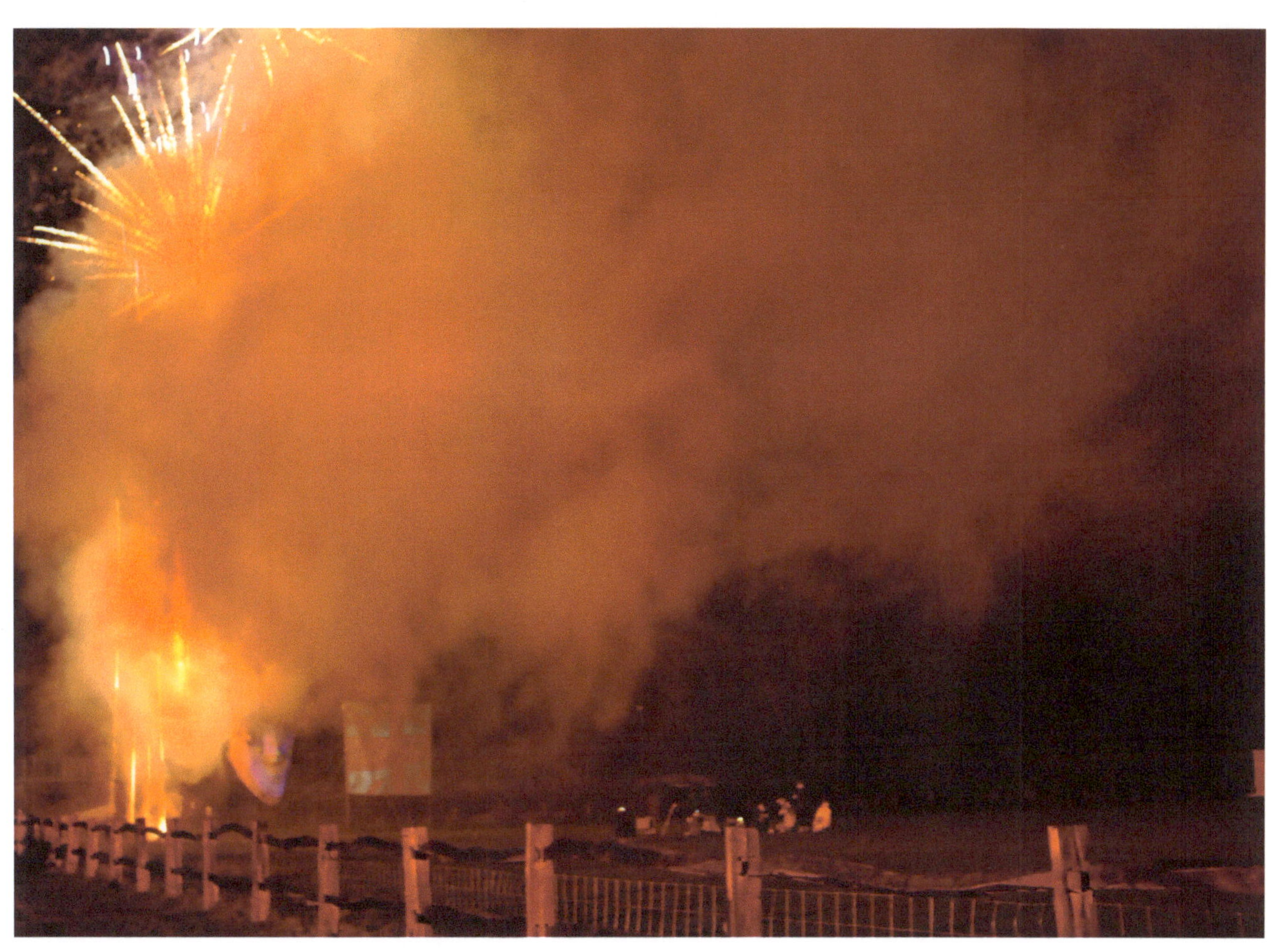

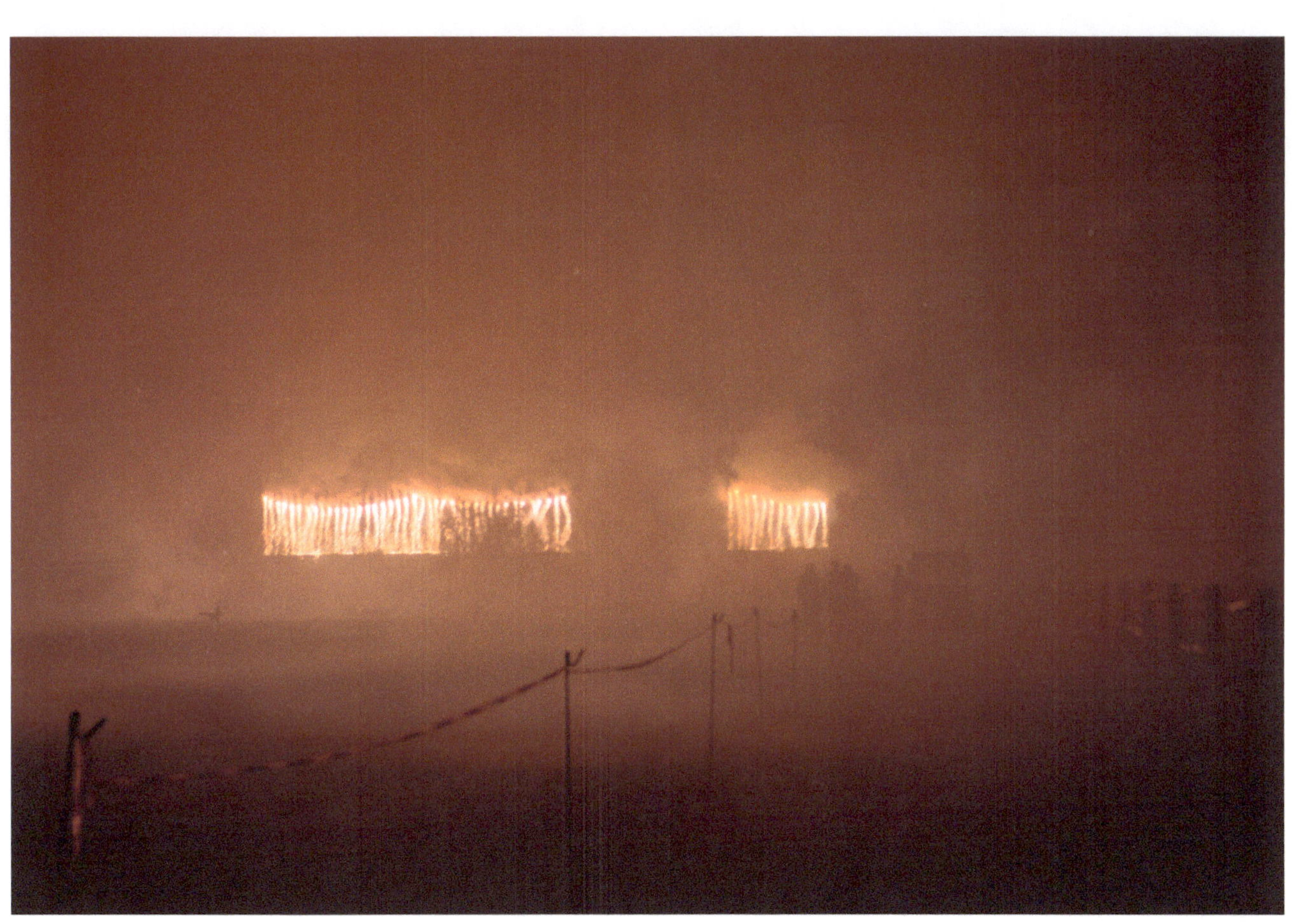

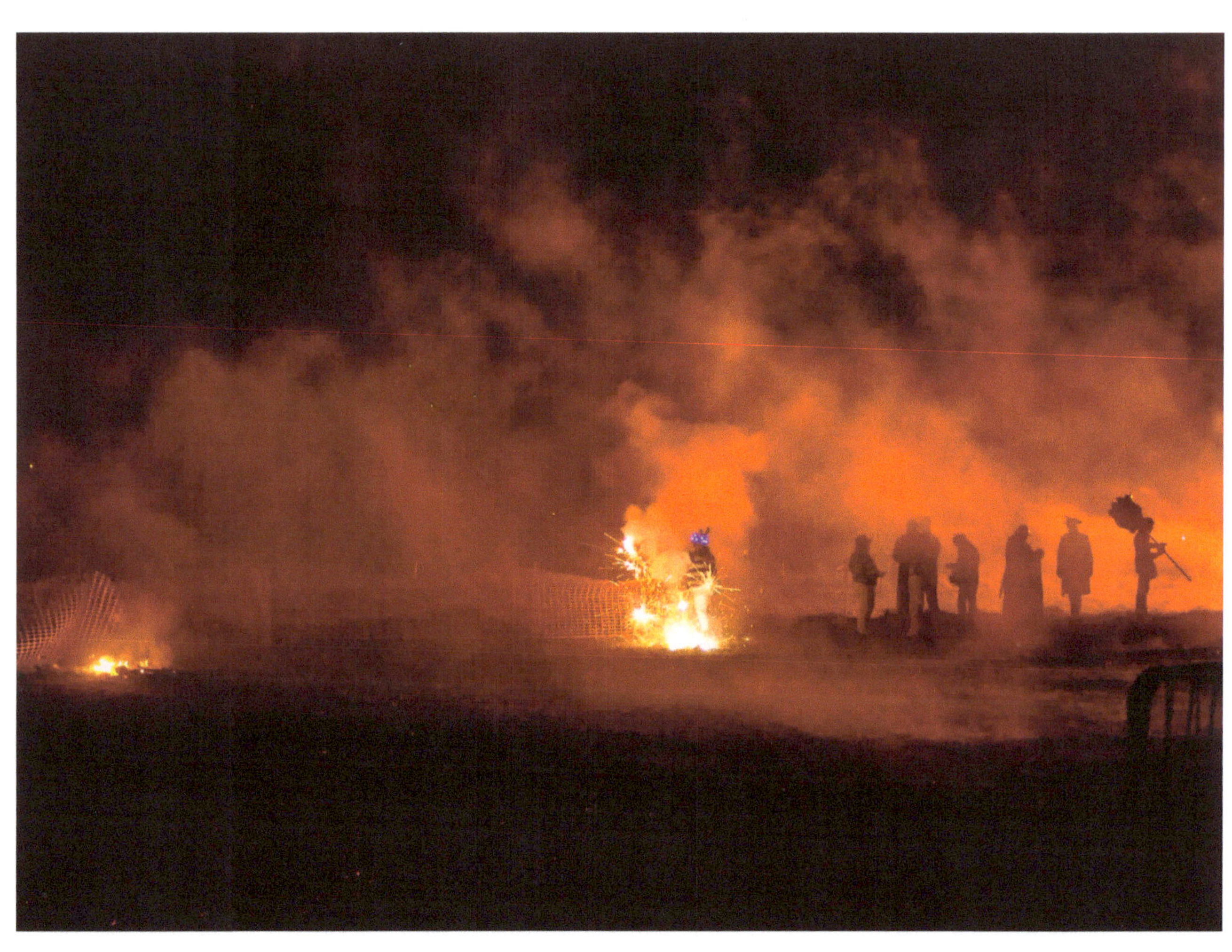

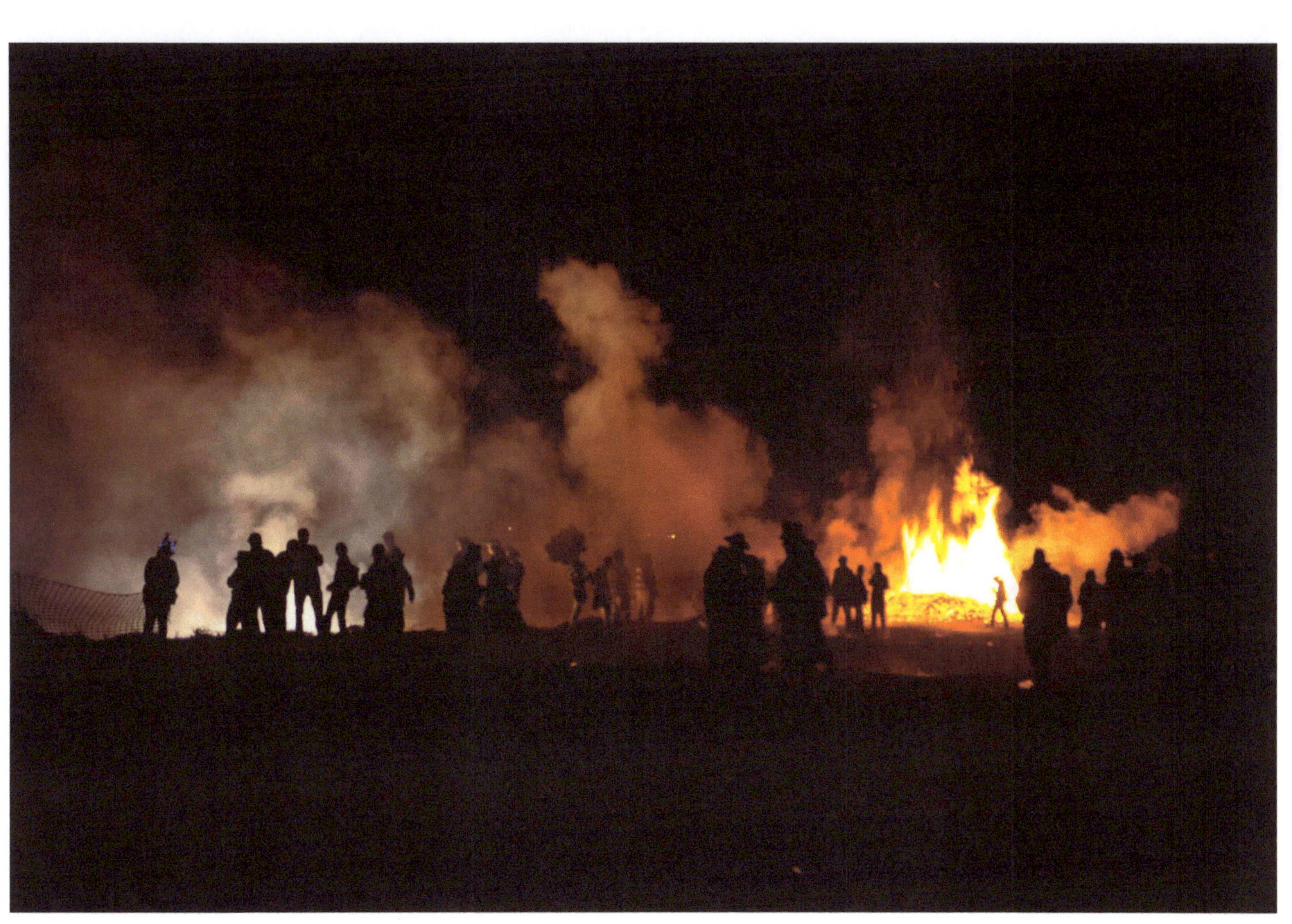

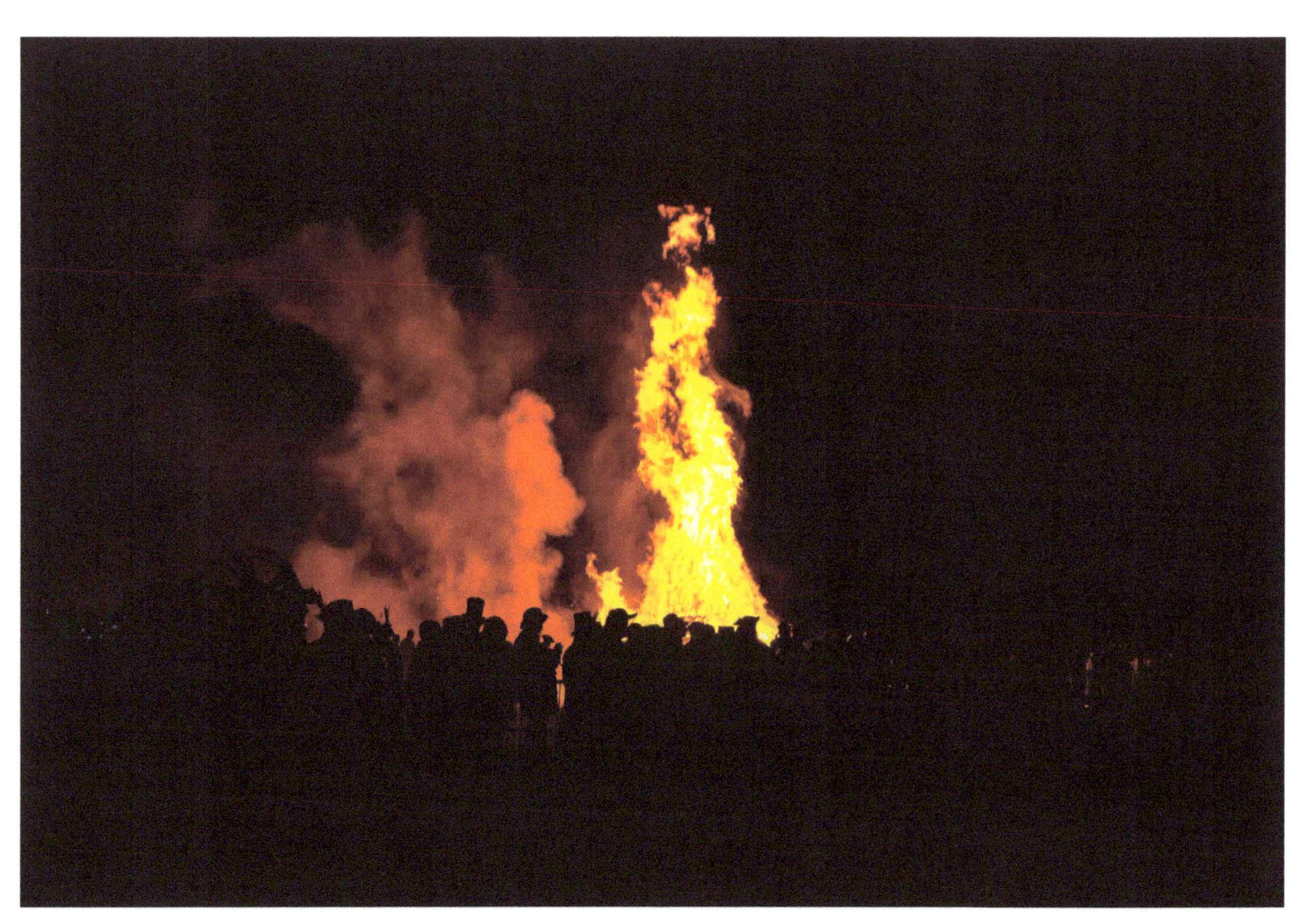

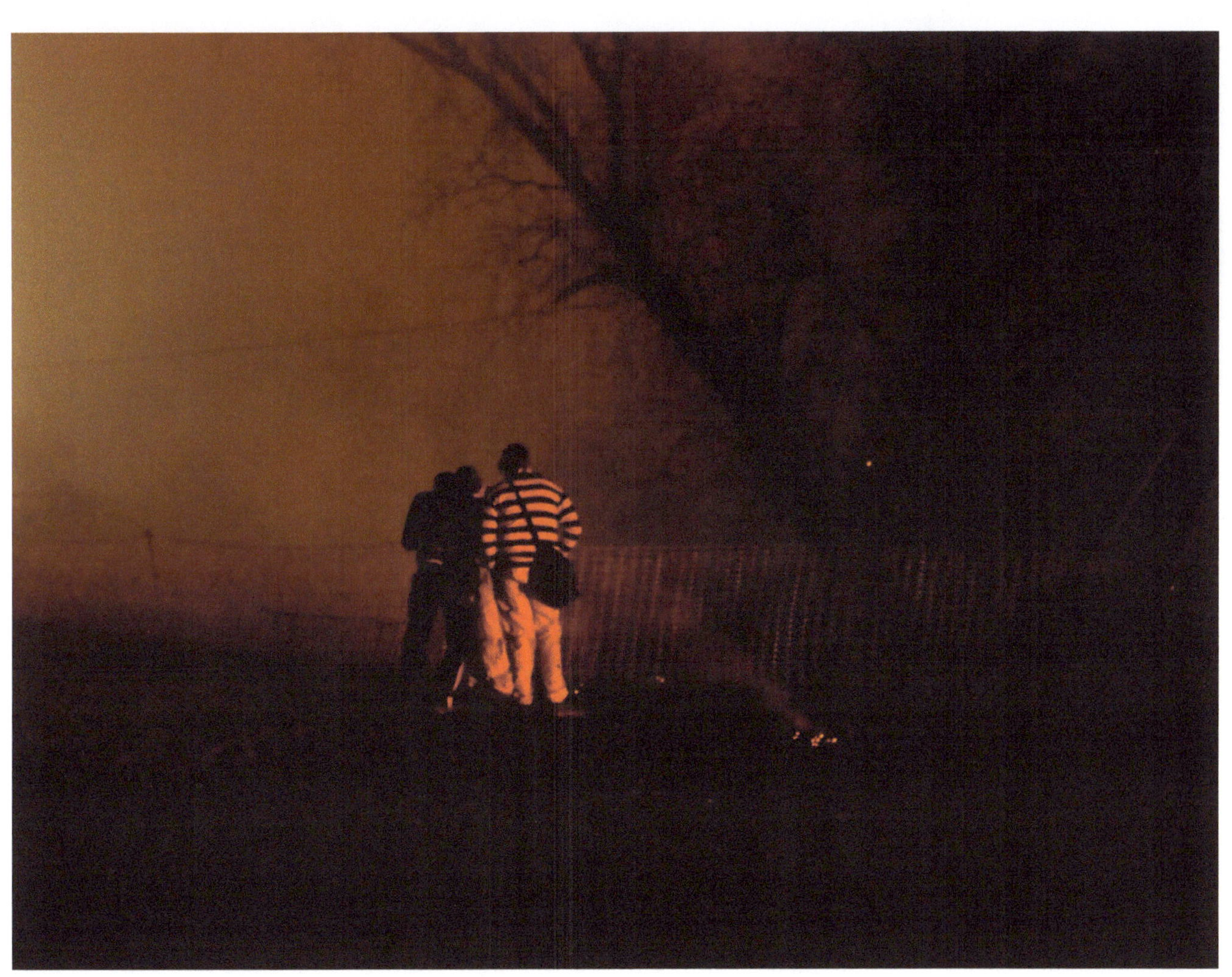

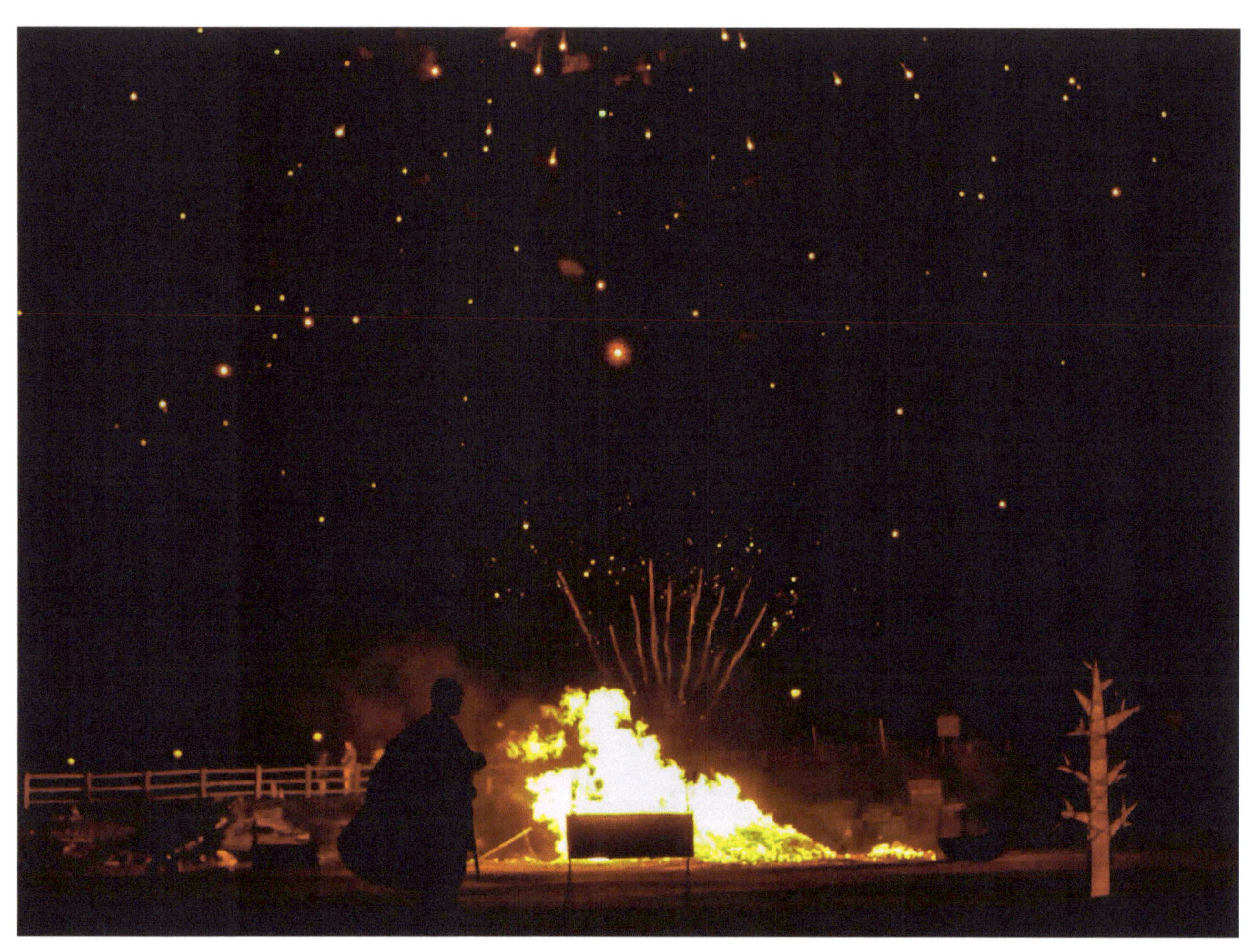

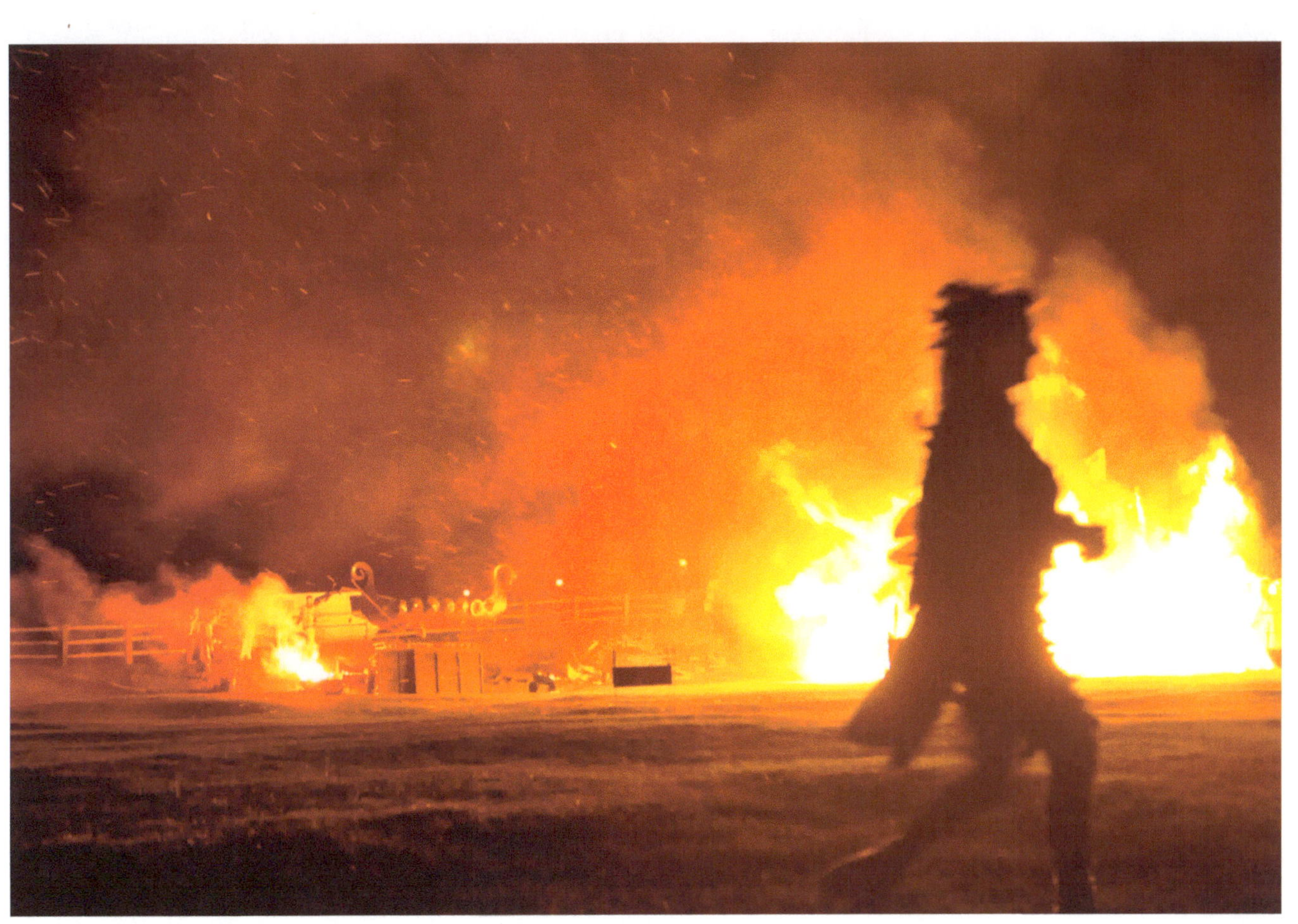

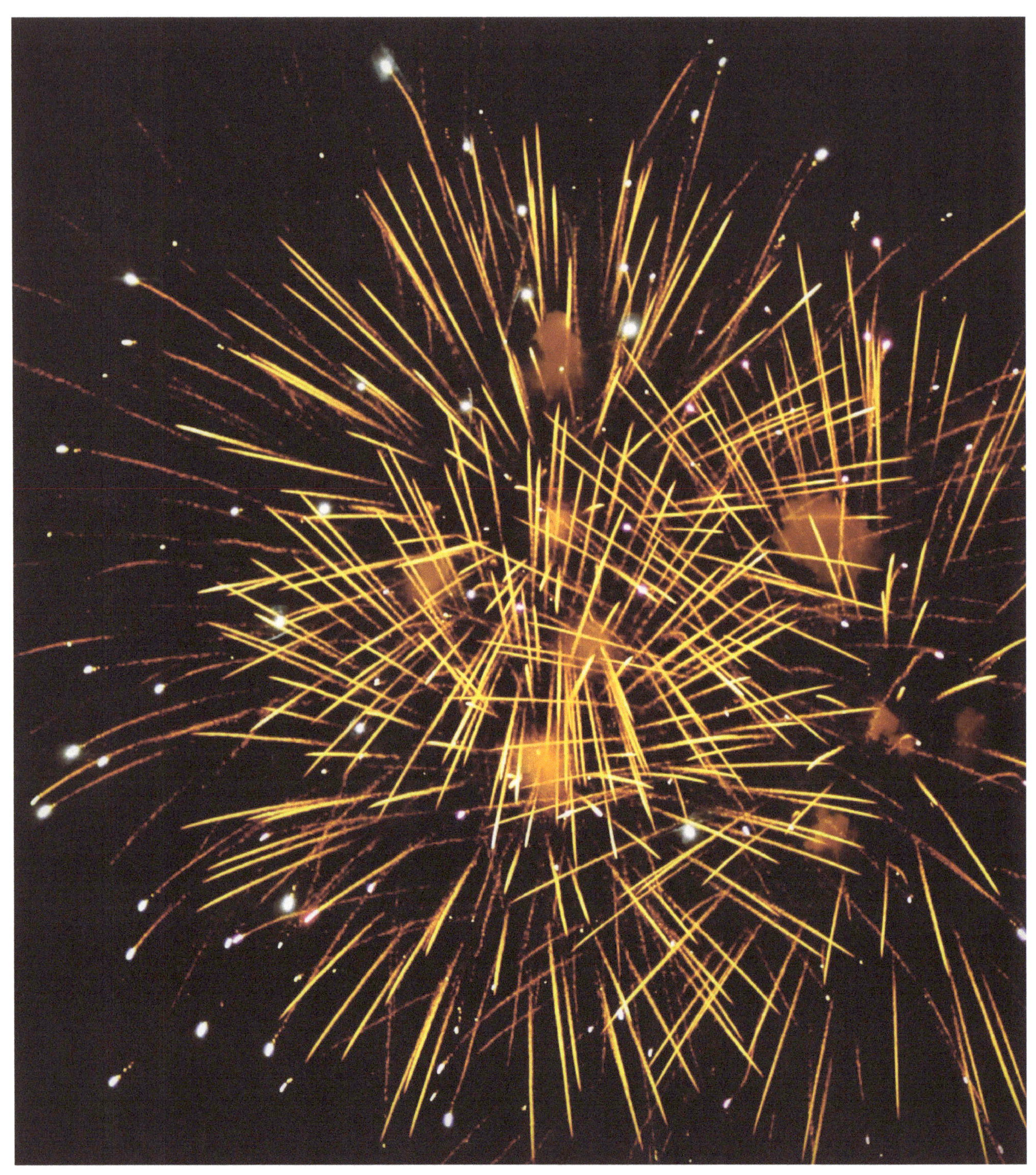

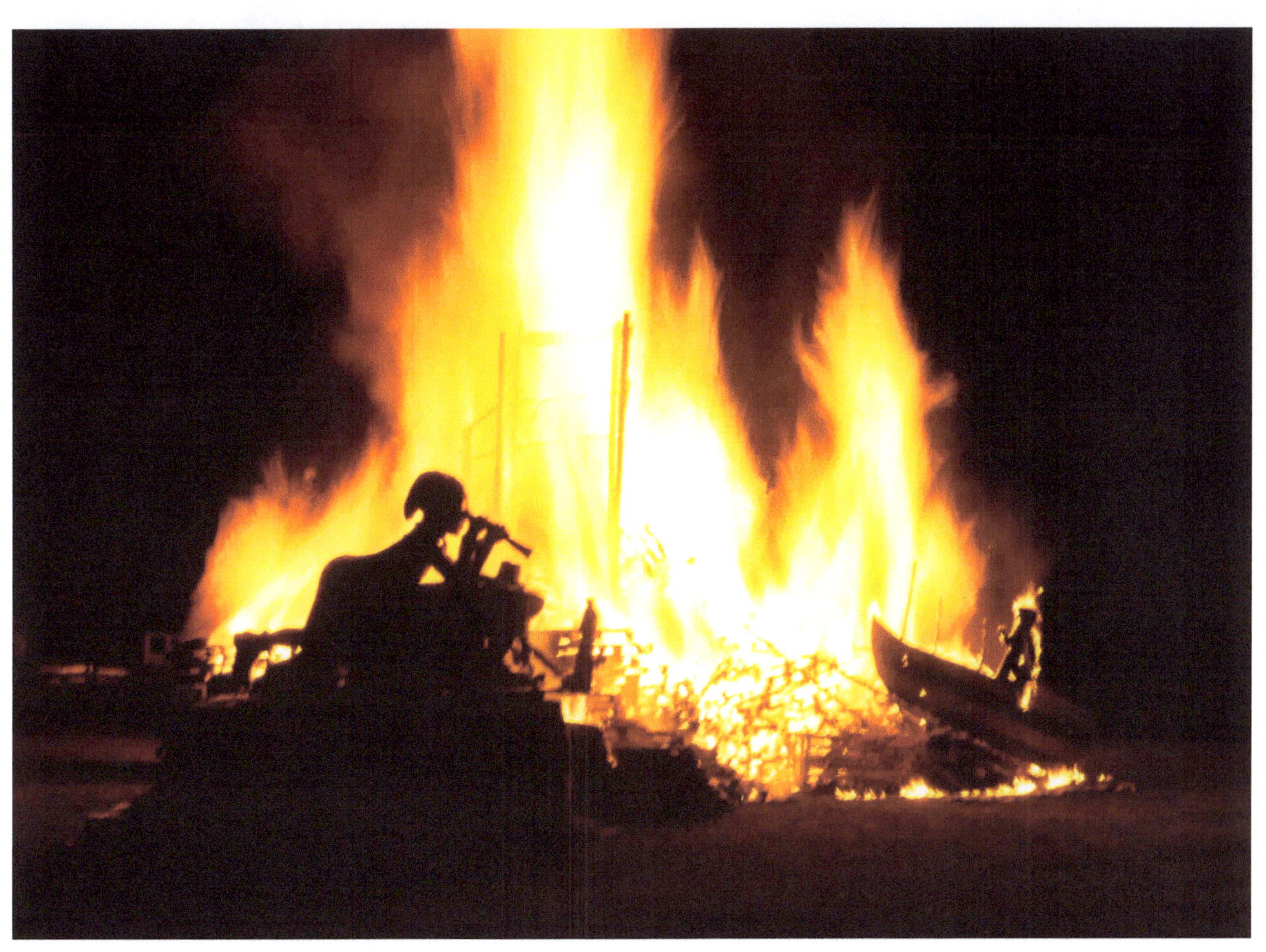

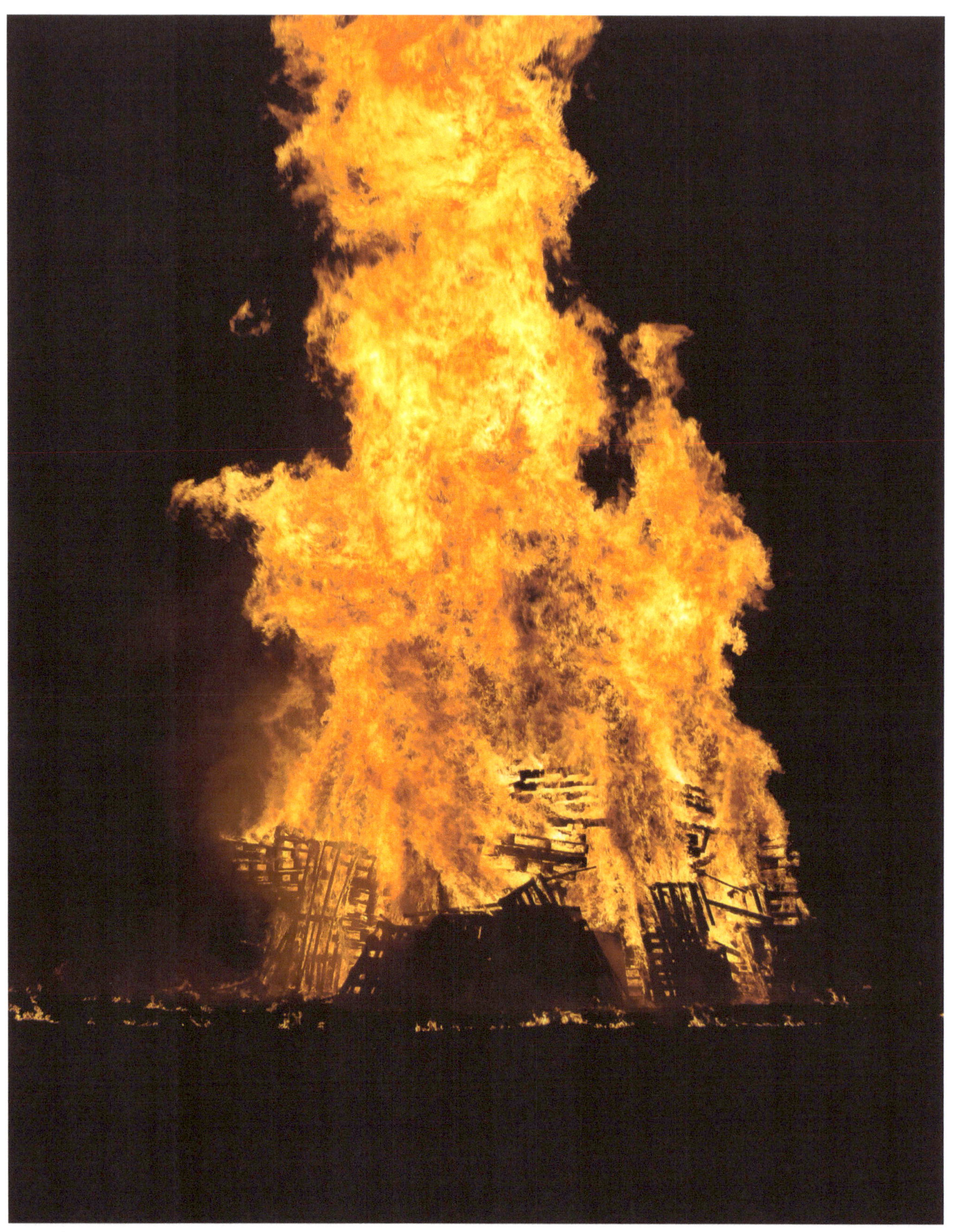

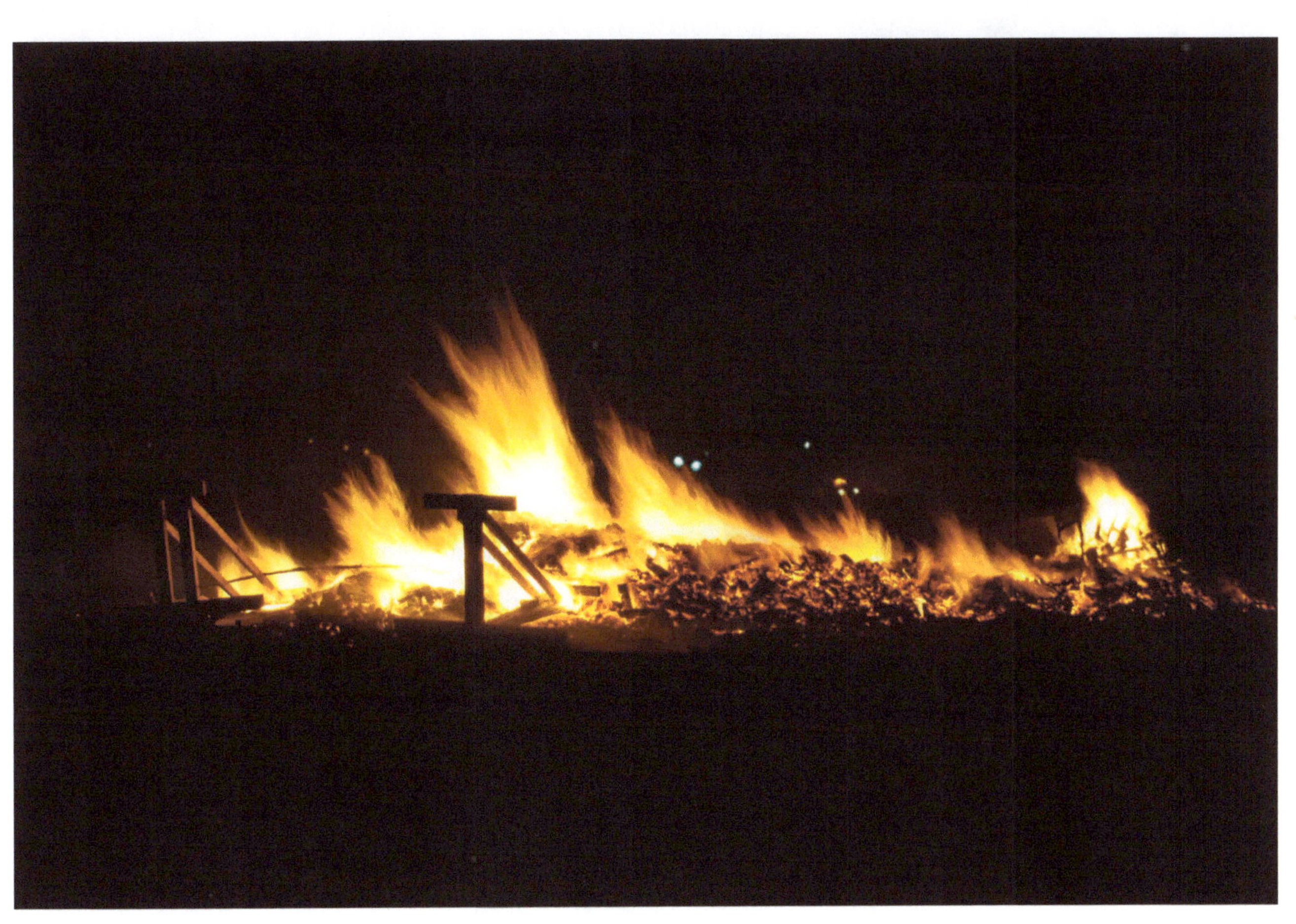

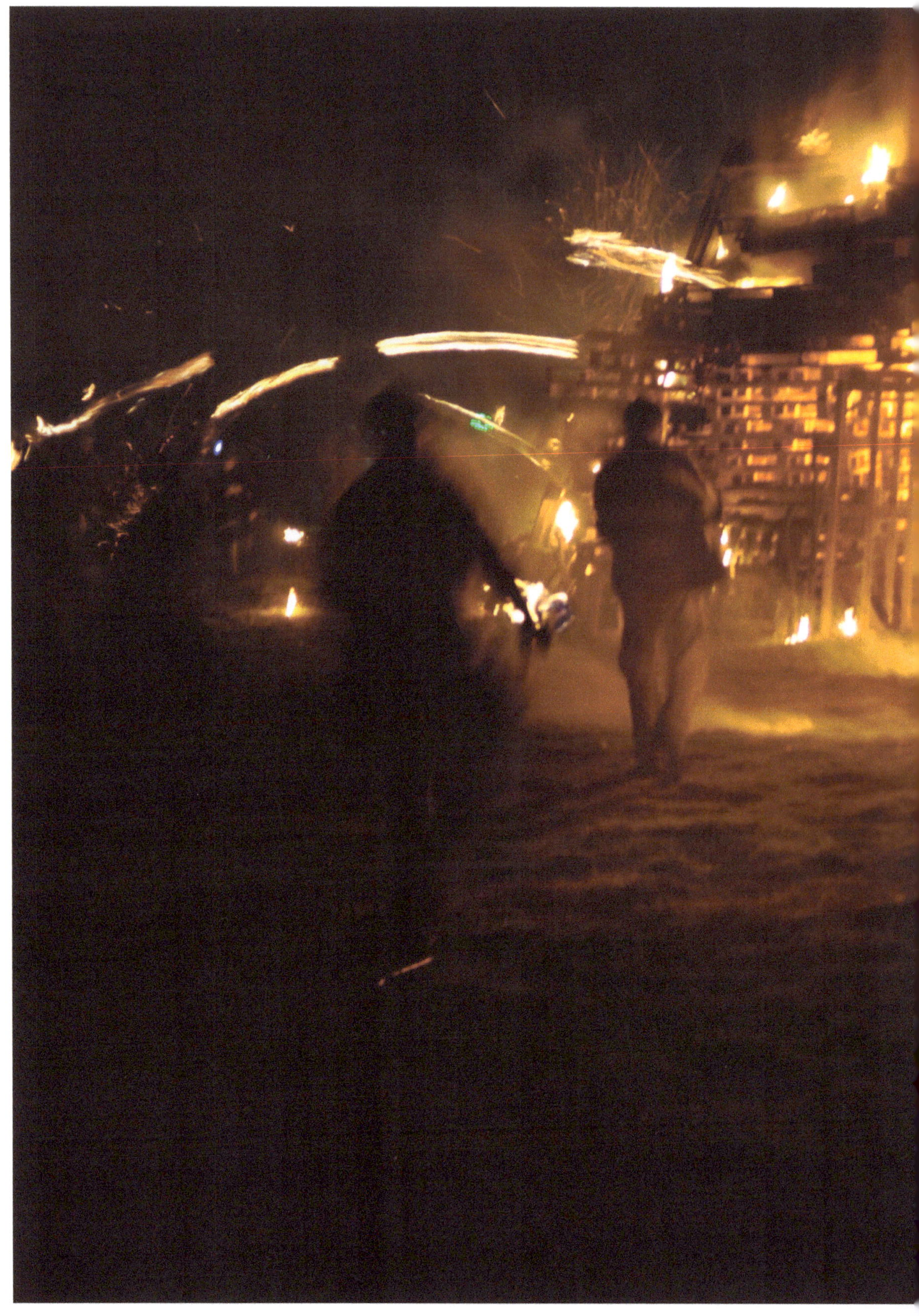

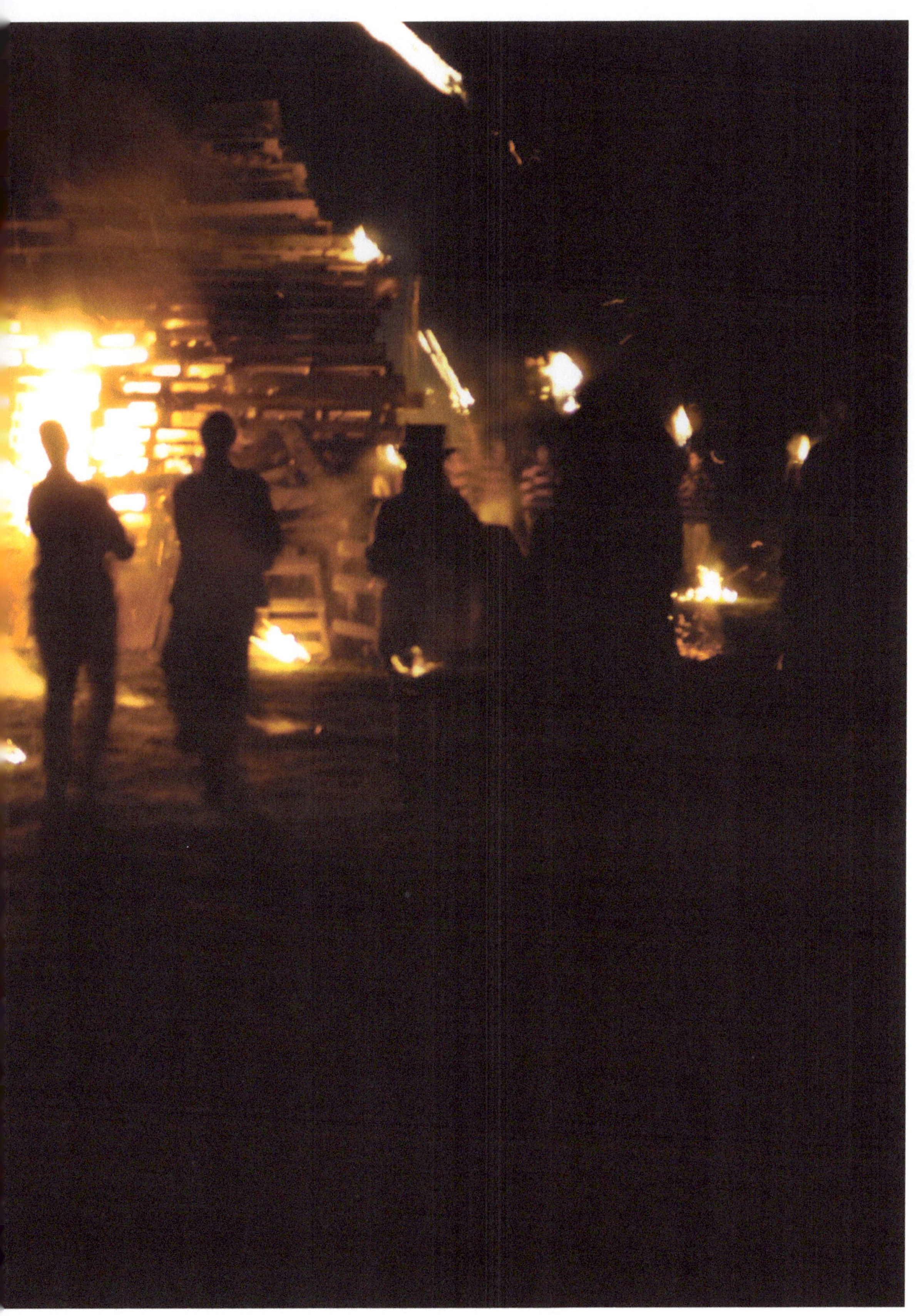

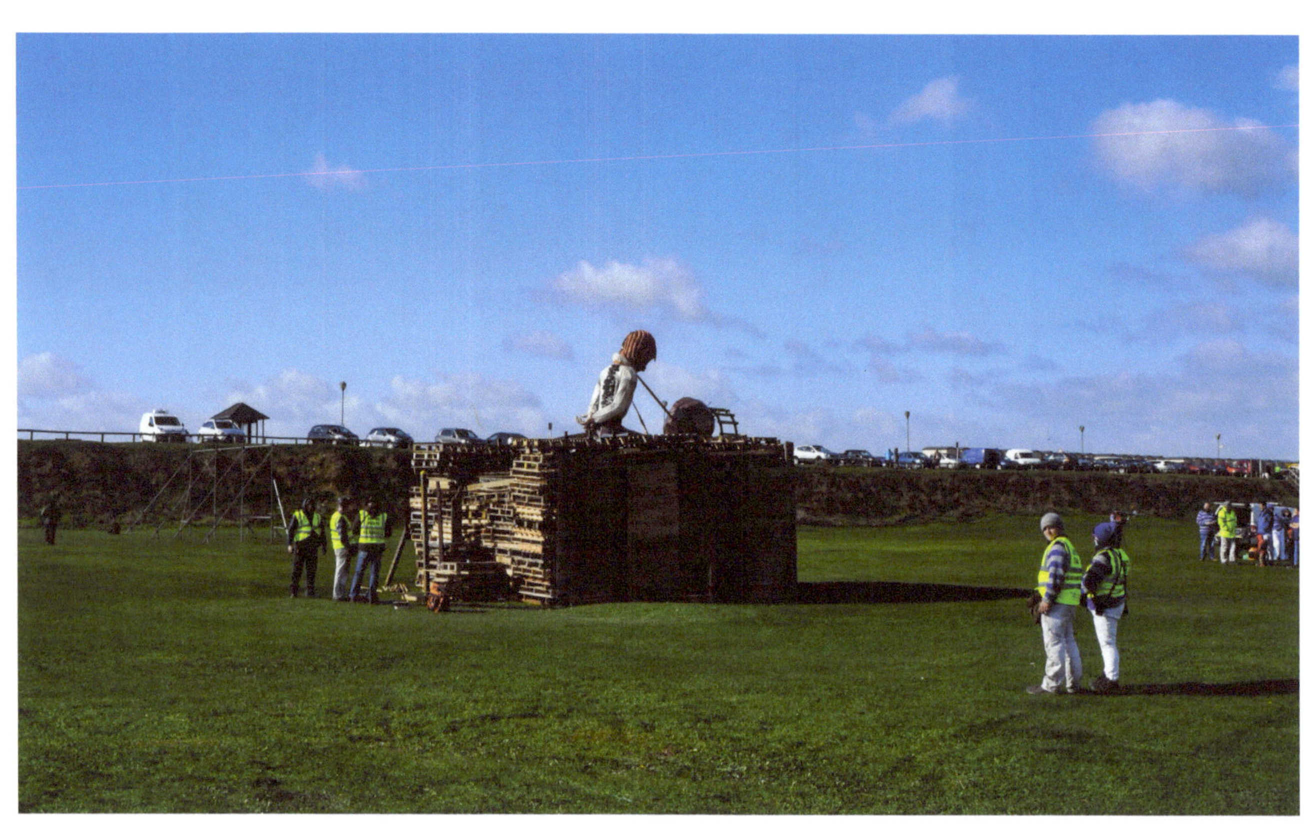

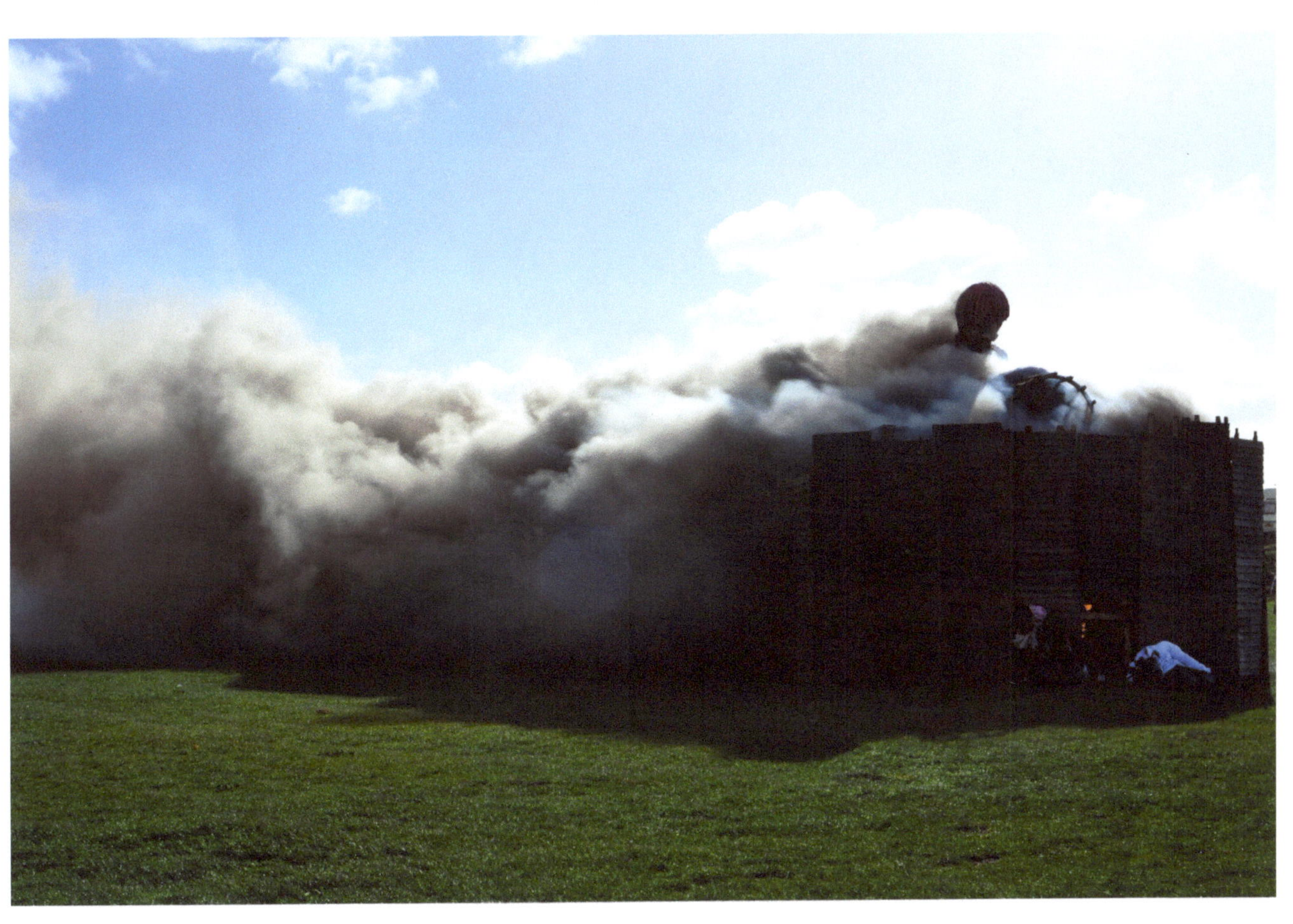

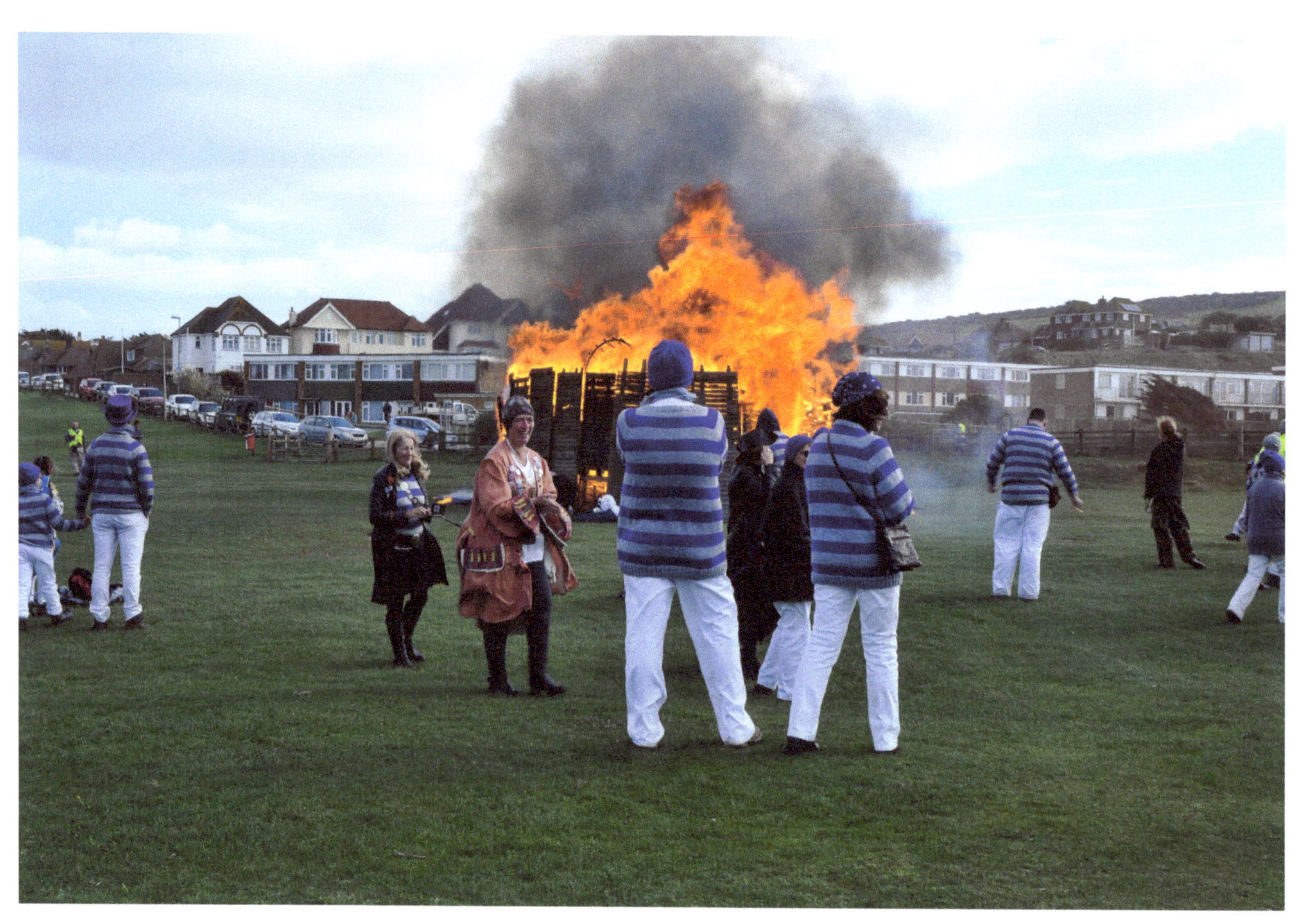

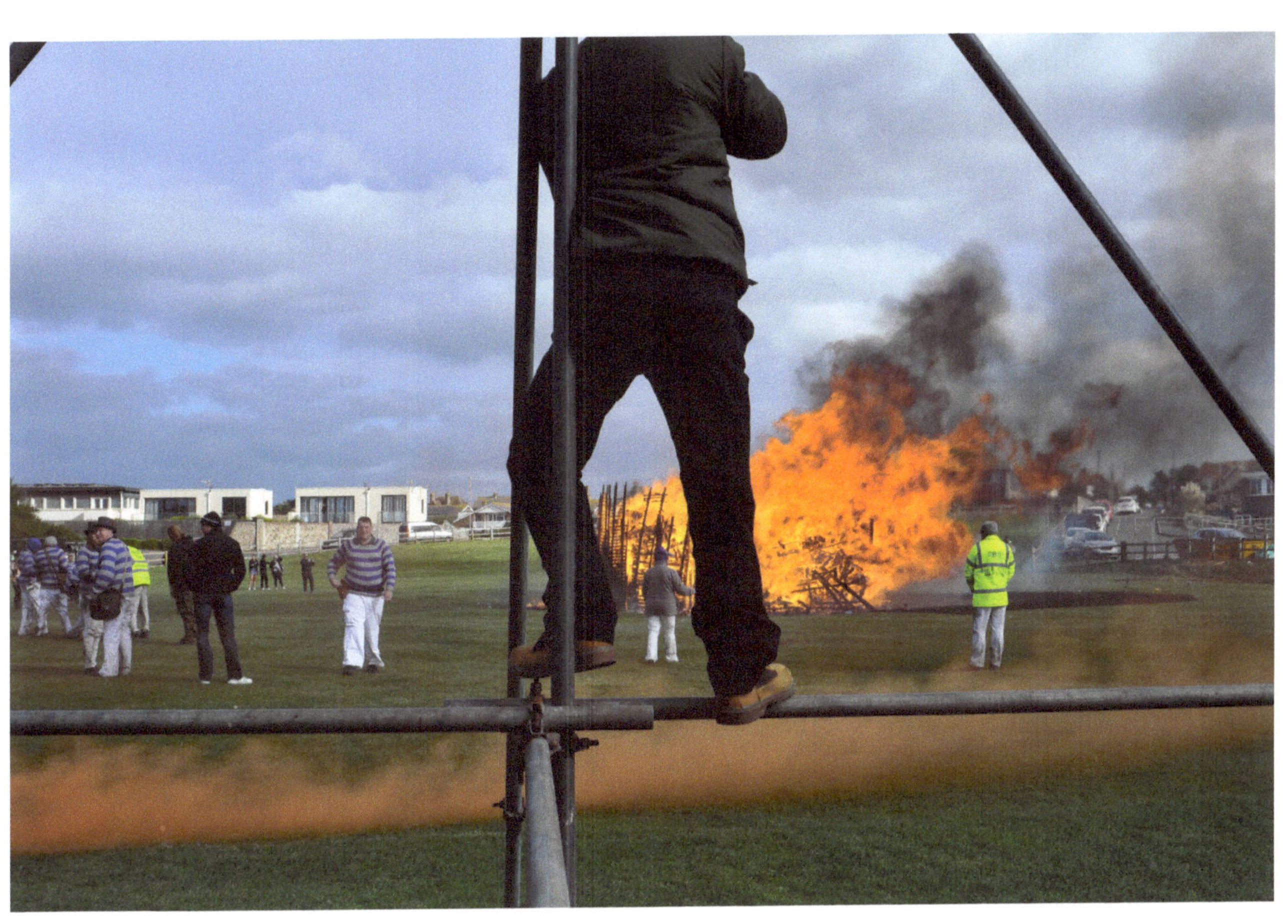

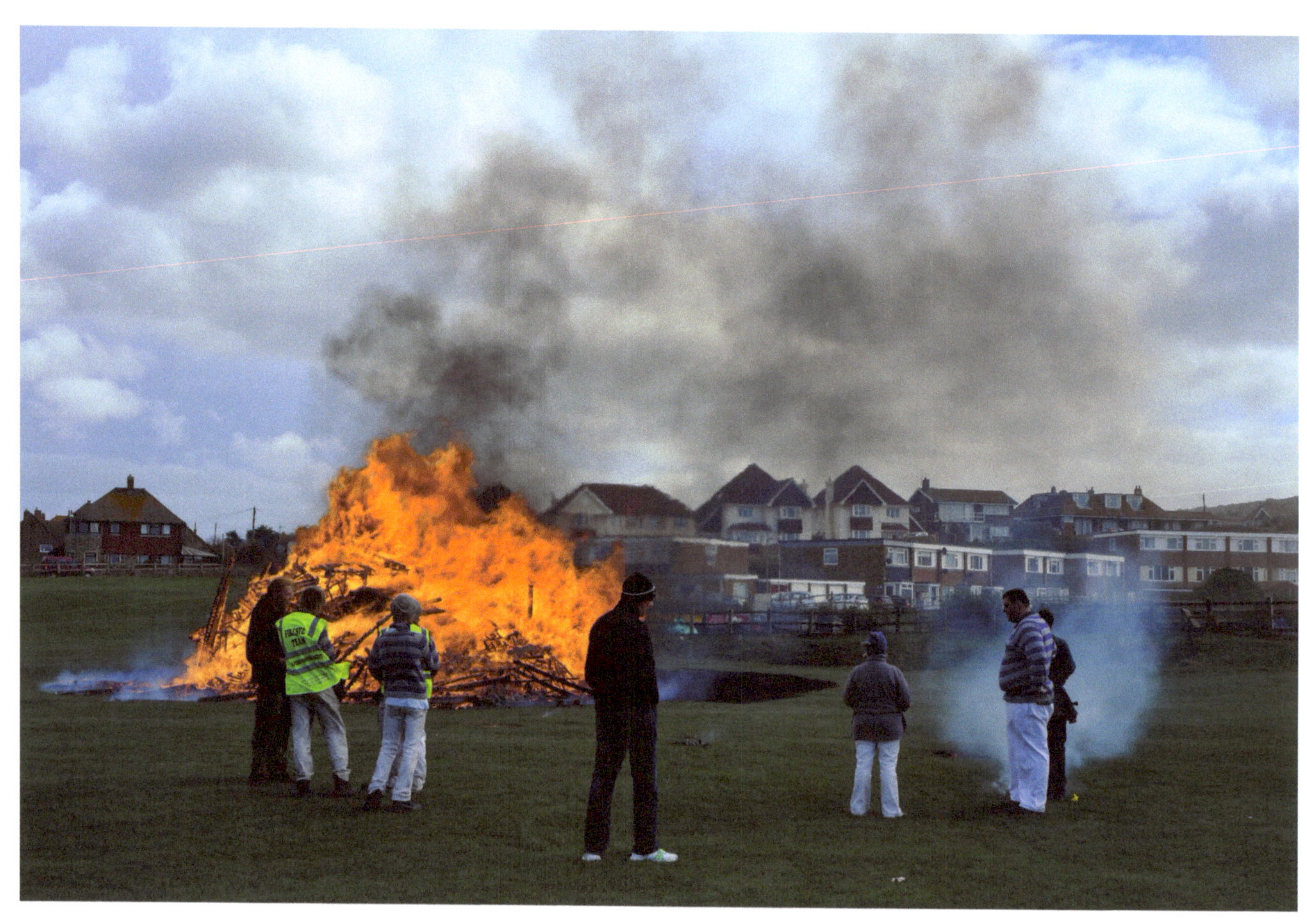

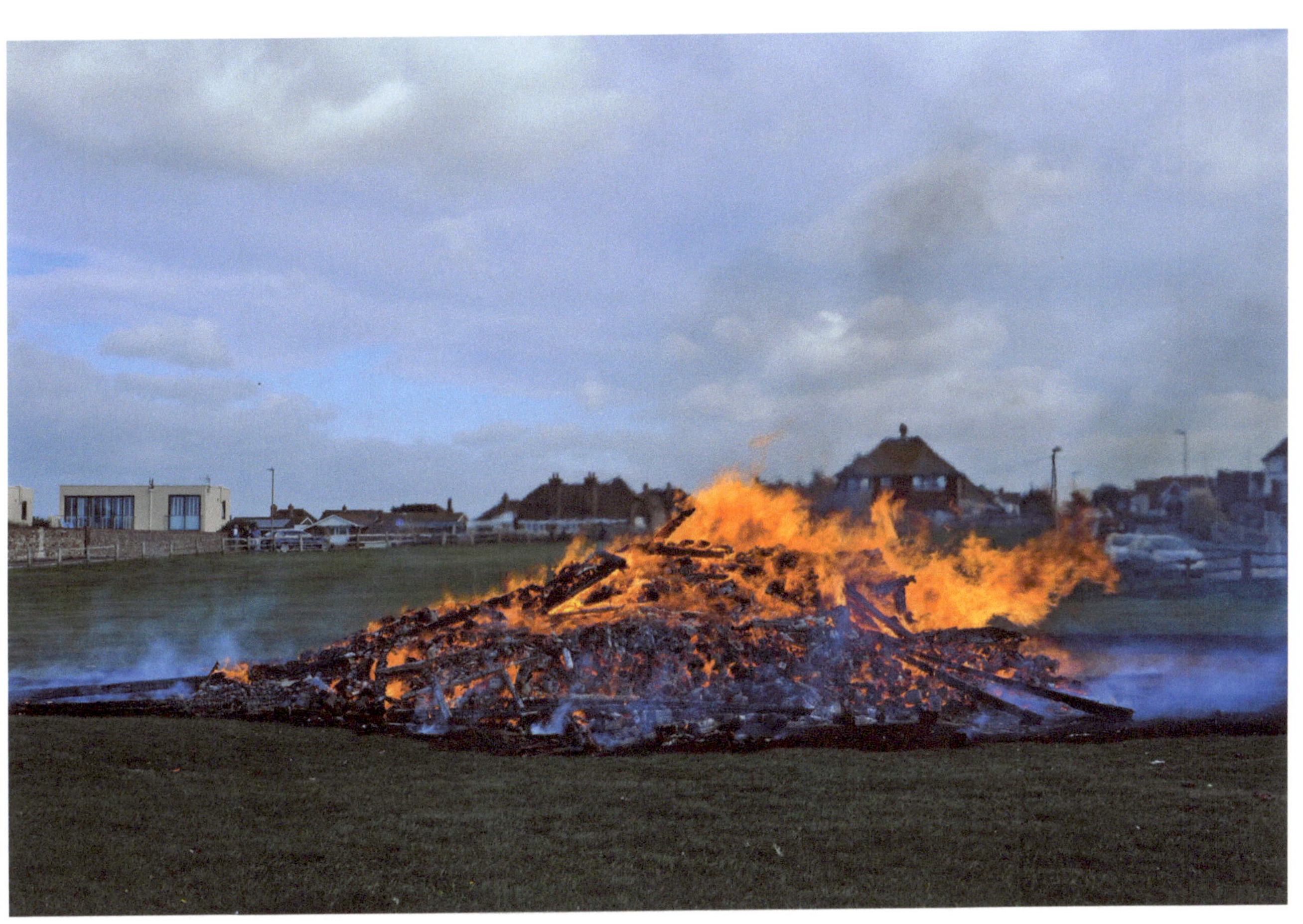

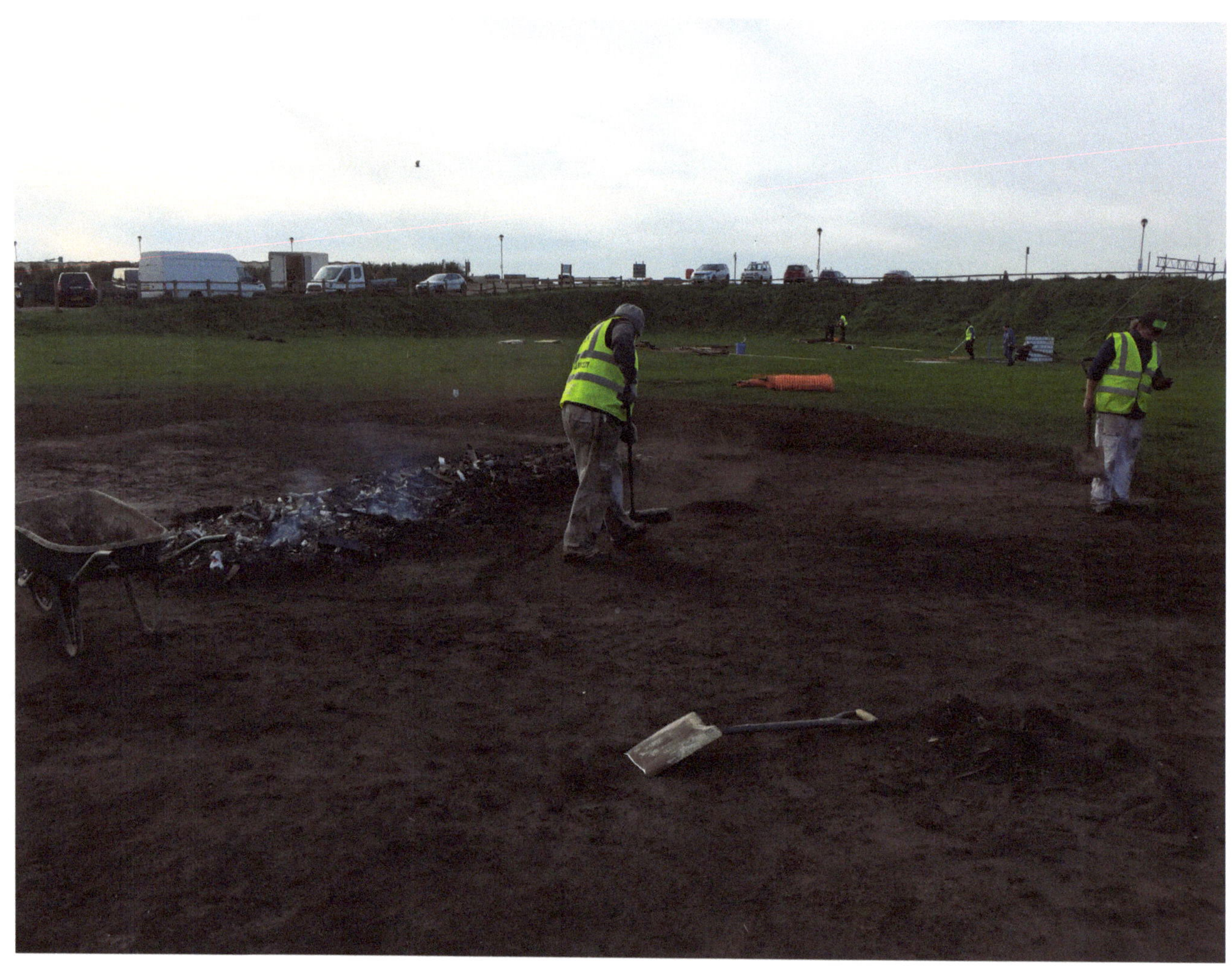

"We burn for good"

Sussex bonfire motto

List of Works